REFLECTIONS
ON MY
JOURNEY OF
FAITH
MOVING CLOSER TO MY DESTINATION

REFLECTIONS
ON MY
JOURNEY OF
FAITH
MOVING CLOSER TO MY DESTINATION

*Psalm 127:1a Unless the LORD build the house,
they labor in vain who build.* *

BELZA ELIA RAMOS

XULON PRESS

Xulon Press
2301 Lucien Way #415
Maitland, FL 32751
407.339.4217
www.xulonpress.com

"Build the path by walking" is an old saying in the public domain. It is used in Africa. There is a similar one in Spanish: *Iba abriendo brechas*." He/she was going opening trails."

Printed in the United States of America.

Paperback ISBN-13: 978-1-6628-0198-3
Ebook ISBN-13: 978-1-6628-0199-0

TABLE OF CONTENTS

INTRODUCTION

Psalm 127:1a Unless *the LORD build the house, they labor in vain who build.* *

T his book is about my journey of faith and redemption. As a cradle Catholic I "knew" of God, but sadly put Him on a shelf for thirteen years. This long period was sad not only because I was in a disastrous marriage, but because it separated me from Him. Not receiving the Eucharist at Mass broke my heart and confused my children, who are baptized and confirmed. I yearned to go back to my faith, as immature and unschooled as it had been and yearned "being church".

Thanks to God and my parents, the foundation had been laid and God was ever tugging at my heart to come back. By His grace, I got out of the "sad situation" and surrounded myself with family, supportive friends and colleagues. The Church had reformed itself post Vatican II, and lay people could have a greater role in parish life. With the humility of having been "fallen and separated" it met my needs. I cannot get enough learning about what being church as a Catholic means. Angels in my path helped me take the next important step: Reconciliation and Eucharist.

I needed to develop a **relationship** with Christ and learn to follow Him. I needed to meet the Holy Spirit and listen. Three things that helped me were: 1. Learning who the Holy Spirit is and does, and 2. Learning how He and Christ work in my life, and 3. Getting involved with Small Christian Communities (SCCs). I share how SCCs transform lives and did mine. We move Christ, the Word, from our heart and let Him use us as His hands, feet, ears, mouth to do His work and let Him work in us.

Compiling twenty years of writings into the orderly sequence of a journey was difficult, but I was called to share them. Scripture, nature and encounters with others inspired these writings. They are only my personal response to God. I leave you, the reader enough room to build your own response. I believe with all my heart, that if you are reading this book it is the reason God was prompting me to share it.

DEDICATION

To my parents, Don Antonio and Doña Panchita, who brought me up to love God, family and country and how that translates into actions. Rest in Peace.

To Father Healey, whom I met when I was making the path by walking it. Also to all my Brothers and Sisters in Christ who through Small Christian Communities, locally, nationally and globally, have become my extended family on my journey, as we seek to strengthen our faith.

To all the members of The Next Chapter (TNC) formerly Las Mujeres and Writing With Angels (WWA) where the idea of writing three books was born. In TNC we all found our voices, a certainty that our life stories were powerful and must be written for posterity. In WWA I found inspiration in The Word and the idea that my faith journey is a story in itself, took life.

To my son and daughter who have lived it all with me and probably view it from their own perspectives. To my grandchildren, who at some time in the future may want to know something or clarify a fuzzy memory of Abuela, I hope you find an answer here.

To you the Reader. Know that there is purpose in all you do and there is a God who is lovingly waiting for us with open arms. May there be something in this book that speaks deeply to you.

ACKNOWLEDGEMENTS

This is a non-fiction faith-based book, therefore all material included, except for Bible scripture quotes cited as inspiration for the poem or story that accompanies it, is original to the author.

Permission for Bible quotes is given on the website of the New American Bible Foundation. No written permission is required for the amount of material used in this book.

"Build the path by walking." is an old proverb, probably African, quoted often by members of my SKYPE Small Christian Community who are African, but my parents also quoted a similar one in Spanish: "*Iba abriendo brechas,*" (S/He walked as s/he opened the trail.")

The names of persons referred to or quoted in this work are true names, unless otherwise stated. If the person is living, I have their verbal agreement to use their name.

All photographs used are originally taken by and belong to the author and if titled, are titled for the piece that accompanies it. The same photo may be an inspiration for more pieces and maybe retitled.

I give special credit to my son, Tony Long, for all his technical help with formatting the pictures to comply with Xulon requirements, and resolving all computer glitches encountered.

1

FAITH FOUNDATIONS:
GOOD ROLE MODELS

Boundless Mother Love *

Mama Panchita and Papa had twelve children, but only six of us survived to adulthood. I am the youngest of all. In the early 1920's when they married at 23 and 17, life was hard in Salineño, TX, which lacked electricity and running water until after Falcon Dam was completed in 1953. Mother and infant mortality were high, diseases were endemic to the area. My parents took in several orphaned or displaced children. Neither of my parents was raised with a mother and father.

My mother was raised by her half-brother and unmarried half-sister, who were grown and had children my mother's age. When I did family research, I asked her why her mother left her with them, but she just said, *"Mi'ja, Deja los muertos muertos y lo pasado en el pasado."*

When I insisted, she said, *"Me crie como la Cenicienta,"* which I understand that she was *"la criada"*, like Cinderella, a maid in her household, and wanted to leave all that in the past and dead actors, dead. I know that Mama reunited with my grandmother and that there was reconciliation if any was needed. We got to know Mama Merced, truly our Abuela.

My father's mother died at childbirth and he was raised by his grandmother when his father remarried. My parents had a big heart and believed that family is sacred. They were not bitter toward anyone, loved their family and taught us to love them too.

My father left Salineño at 17 to work for the MKT Railroad and returned at 23. He and my mother married in 1920. When Carmen, my oldest sister was born in 1922, my parents took in my father's cousin's four orphaned children, three boys and an infant girl, Mareita. My mother was 19.

In 2002 when Carmen was living with me, that infant girl, Mareíta, now 80, had her daughter, Jisa, contact me. We all had moved out of Salineño and lost contact for many years. Mareita told me that she wanted to get together with us so that my Mother in heaven would know that she was not "*una ingrata*", not an ingrate. Jisa and I made sure we got them together often. They both loved casinos and we even took them once.

Belza, Mareita, Carmen

Other children were taken in for short periods of time, for varying reasons. Some were reclaimed by grandparents once they were old enough to go to school and help the family work in the fields. This was before I was born, but my brothers told me my mother suffered when these children were taken from her. She also suffered when she lost three babies before they were two years old and three newborns within hours of birth. They were "water babies" a condition common when the mother has gestational diabetes. Encephalitis and dysentery took the other three. I know that all the surrogate siblings loved my parents, visited regularly and maintain contact with us.

My parents were Don Antonio and Doña Panchita, titles of respect, to all who knew them. They were good role models as parents, neighbors and citizens in the public arena. Mama prepared every child in Salineño for First Communion and Confirmation, and I became her assistant after my First Communion. Papa told me that when women got the right to vote, my mother, not of age to vote herself, taught women to vote with sample ballots. Both shared what little they had with those in greater need. They also shared their God-given talents with family and neighbors. Frequently, they involved me to deliver their generosity to one family or another: a basket of Mama's baking or hand sewn baby clothes for a newborn, fruits and vegetables Papa harvested. If there had been a death or new birth, or illness or other calamity, they knew they needed help. My father's advice or help was sought by young farmers.

At her funeral Mass in 1993, several young men spoke reverently about being who they are today because Doña Panchita taught them to read and write so they could join the Army. She had started them on their spiritual journey, they said, and by getting into the army with her help, they benefitted from the GI Bill to learn a trade. Many women remembered that Mama taught them how to take care of their newborn babies, sew and knit. She taught them to make quilts, tamales and crafts. Mama also had some basic nursing skills, like giving shots, catheterizing, bringing a fever down and applying poultices or making teas with different herbs for different injuries or illnesses. She was often summoned at all hours to come to the aid of an ill or dying neighbor. Besides making herbal teas and giving other care, she always had the right Bible verse and prayers to give hope and to console.

It was only natural that I would follow their example and get involved in my own community and church work. When we moved to Corpus Christi, I started volunteering as a Candy Striper in the public hospital at fifteen. I have taught English and citizenship classes to immigrants through my parish, participated in voter registration drives, taught Red Cross Mother and Baby Care classes for expectant parents, and more. I was involved with United Way over thirty years in Corpus Christi and Dallas. For thirty years I coordinated the formation of Small Christian Communities in my parishes in Dallas and then in San Antonio. I am a Lector, have been a presenter, table leader or planning team member in several ongoing parish courses or studies.

Humbly, I have to say it's been much easier for me than it must have been for my parents. Because they encouraged me to get an education, I was better prepared to follow their example and to forge new careers to deal with the unexpected turns in my life. They instilled in me the values that have guided me throughout my life. Mil gracias Diosito.

Parents, Francisca and Antonio

(Note: Five of us from The Next Chapter Writing Group, read our stories on Texas Matters on Texas Public Radio, circa 2006, and they aired several years before Mother's Day. I read a very similar version of "Boundless Mother Love".)

God, the Farmer

My father was like most men in our small village. He did not attend church regularly and only went for our Baptisms, First Communions, and Confirmations and sometimes Easter and Christmas. However, he had ongoing conversations with God, like he would with another farmer, except that my father expected more from God. Papa was a born farmer in touch with nature, sensitive to the weather. He spent most of the week at his ranch, close to three miles away from our village. In South Texas, God needed to cooperate with rain and control the Northers that blew in with sudden frost.

Papa was profoundly moved by the sprouting of seeds he planted or the birth of a new foal or any of his farm animals and gave God credit. He thanked God for a good crop.

"God, it's time to plant; and we'll need some rain soon after. Send us slow, steady rain because hard rain just runs off to the gullies, seeds and all."

My father appealed to Mother Mary as to his mother who died when he was born. Once when he was home it started hailing. He asked Mother Mary that Her Son protect his crops at the ranch. He went out when the hail stopped and brought in an egg shaped hail stone. He was all excited, certain it had not hailed at the ranch. He showed us the hail stone in proof. It was absolutely clear ice, except that in the center there was a milky white full body image of Mary, with praying hands, mantle, even a sash. We all examined it and my mother said we must get on our knees and pray the rosary. My father stood with a smile on his thin lips, but he did not join in audibly.

After the rosary, he and my brother quickly saddled the horses and took off to the ranch. Sure enough, they came back to tell us the crops and animals were fine.

My brother remembers how one day they were resting on the ground at the ranch. They suddenly felt the earth vibrating with a loud, distant rumbling, like a cattle stampede. My father jumped up saying, *"Ave María Purísima, esperanos, que tenemos que mover los animales a la loma".* He asked Mary for time for them to get the animals and themselves safely to higher ground before the wave of water roared by. Papa had experienced this rare phenomenon before, and explained to my brother that it was the earth's layers shifting, releasing pressure at the core, that created a geyser of hot water. With the terrain being so flat, the water travels for miles like a tsunami gathering momentum and debris, animals and humans.

I saw my father praying on his knees only once – in the middle of our lot by the Rio Grande. We had gone down several times to monitor the river rising. The water was half way up the tall bank on our side and covering the trees on the Mexican side, and still rising. We saw houses, people, animals dead and alive, whole trees and branches floating by – destruction creating more destruction. We walked back up to our house. He and my brothers had already tied it to the strongest trees in our lot and moved the haystacks to the ranch the day before. He knelt on the ground, praying to God. That night he rested by the back door, hand dangling out. We were all ready to leave for higher ground on his word.

Sometimes I wonder if my father is giving God some advice in Heaven or bargaining with him. Maybe they just talk about planting seeds on fertile ground.

Un Gran Hombre – Mi Papa

Papa came in to the kitchen and cut off Bobby Darin "Splishin' N' Splashin'" on the radio. Like countless times before, he sat down, asking "What are you studying?"

"I am studying Constitutional Rights." I answered, refrained from asking "Why did you turn off the radio?"

I knew we were in for a l-o-n-g discussion, especially if we disagreed on something, which was often. He would get angry; I would try to reason with him. He would get angrier and become more unreasonable. (Where did a daughter of his get those ideas; how dare she contradict him?) Of course, our *pleitos* had nothing to do with reason. He would never, ever concede "You're right", but deep down, I felt he was proud I had a mind of my own. Since we had moved from Salineño to Corpus Christi, we were both like little fish "splishin' n' splashin" in a big pond. I was discovering new ideas in the big city through friends and school. But he and Mama warned "be careful, these children were not raised like you". Papa became even more controlling, Mama more watchful. But then again, this would have happen anyway, because I was now fifteen.

On the other hand, I was proud of Papa's self-taught knowledge and liked how he brought my subjects to life with his questions like:

6

What projects were built in South Texas through the Works Projects Administration (WPA)? How did we, *la gente pobre* benefit? Or his stories: Do you know your mother and I were married two months after women got the right to vote in the US? I did not see her for months as she went around with sample ballots teaching women to vote in the county elections. Or, how Montezuma appealed to his brother not to break down under torture and squeal? "*¿A caso crees que yo estoy en un lecho de rosas?*"

Life with a third grade education and a bad temper had not been a bed of roses for Papa either. In third grade, his male teacher threw a tightly wound ball of *sisal* (hemp) at him and he threw it back, hitting him at a third grader's height. Children either went to school or worked the fields with their parents. So he helped his father until he left Salineño at seventeen to work for the MKT Railroad for five years.

"Ah, *nuestros derechos ¿*De *dónde vienen?*" he asked. I responded our rights come from God. Papa said they come from the Constitution. Yes, but our forefathers based it on Judeo-Christian principles. (Thank you, God, I thought, when Papa seemed to agree.)

"In order to get your rights, four things are necessary. One, they have to be GRANTED. Two, you have to KNOW what your rights are. Three, you have to CLAIM them. Four, you need to be willing to FIGHT for them."

"Our rights are our rights! No one can deny them to us." I slammed my fist on the table.

"True, but they had to pass the Bill of Rights, didn't they? It made the *gringos* think twice about denying them to *nosotros, los Mejicanos*."

"Papa, *no todo* boils down to the gringos against the *Mejicanos*. Besides we are American." Uh, uh, shouldn't have said that! Most Hispanic original land grantees and their descendants in South Texas feel this way because Anglos stole their land. That was our perpetual argument: his unreasonable anger at gringos.

My older brother Luis had come in with Whataburgers and shakes (our first culinary discovery in the big city) for the three of us and had been listening. He knew we would be up late, as Papa had asked my three older brothers "What are you studying?" throughout all their school years. That's how Papa satisfied his yearning for learning without sacrificing his pride. Luis joined our discussion as we ate, and trying to deflect Papa's brewing anger towards himself, said rights came from his fists and a few choice words. Papa shot that "watch your language look" at him and said: "Let me tell you a story about claiming our rights."

I liked his stories because through them I learned about his life, which helped me understand him, my siblings and myself. Besides, whatever I was studying got embedded in my brain, like fence posts in cement, or the AR singed on our cows rump. As he started the story, I could tell his mind was in the past, with his Papa, whom he also called "Toto". This is his story:

> One day around 1910, I was twelve maybe thirteen, Papa and I were going to *Agualeguas, México* on one horse, carrying an extra saddle. *Un bandido* was stealing horses and cattle along the Texas border and he stole our *Grullo*. The *Rinches* (Rangers) never protected our rights, no use expecting them to look for what was stolen from us. We were going to pick up another work horse so we could plow our land. We had crossed the river and were well into México when we saw a man standing in a field among some horses, his guns glinting in the sun. I recognized our *caballo grullo*.
>
> Toto saw him too and his guns, and warned me *"No, mi'jo ese no es el nuestro."*
>
> I told him "I know our horses and that is ours."
>
> *"Pues déjalo ir.* Let it go. It's getting late and we have a ways to go." *Seguro que* Papa Toto was thinking: *ese bandido* will kill us both.
>
> But I was already heading toward the man. Toto cocked *la veinte-y-dos,* the rifle we always looped to the saddle. *El Grullo* snorted, recognizing me as I walked to him.
>
> I looked the man straight in the eye and said *"Mi nombre es Antonio Ramos. Y estoy seguro, que Usted está seguro que este es mi caballo."*

I led our *Grullo* away by his bit until I got to the road where I mounted him bare back. We continued on our way, not looking back. After a long pause, Papa whispered *"Mi padre solo me dijo: Hombre, si que eres muy testarudo."*

Yes, I too know how stubborn Papa can be, I thought, not failing to catch how his father had granted him passage into manhood by calling him *Hombre*.

"And the *bandido* didn't kill you. You gave him your name, and told him you were sure he was sure this was your horse because he recognized you. Was it because he saw that you were just a child wanting his horse back?" Uh-uh! I could tell he did not like that when his eyes pierced through me.

"Tal vez."

"Or was it because he knew you had a right to that horse?" *"Tal vez."*

"But he never worried about people's rights when he stole. Was it because you acted so brave and with assurance?"

"Tal vez" Papa smiled, sitting even taller, a smile on his thin lips.

Perceiving that he had just wanted the story to teach me about rights, not to reveal anything about himself, I stopped my questioning and returned to my books and Whataburger. Long afterwards, I asked Mama if that story was true.

"O si", she said, "your *abuelo* Toto, told me about it. *Tu Papa siempre a sido muy testarudo*."

To my surprise and hers, I defended him "But can't you see he was also very brave? Mama, why do you think that *bandido* didn't kill Papa?"

She said "*Tal vez* his dead *Mamacita* was looking out for him from heaven."

I can believe that, but have another theory. The *bandido* stole from faceless people in the dark of night, but a mere boy stood up to him, face to face, in bright daylight, identified himself by name, claiming what was rightfully his. That brought things to a personal level, human to human. And Papa had a right to his horse.

As humans, certain inalienable rights have been granted to us by our Creator, recognized in our Constitution. We have to know what our rights are, in order to claim them and if necessary we should be willing to fight for them. God will help us. That is Papa's legacy for his children and grandchildren.

Shaped By Example

Their hands never idle
Dawn to dusk worked in the fields together,
Tended their animals with love and care.
Mama cooked, canned, baked and sewed,
Created crafts to beautify to our simple home,
Papa distributed the fruits of the harvest.
Mama shared her daily yeast rolls and empanadas,
Or a casserole with family or those
Who "had come upon hard times".
Papa trained a neighbor's horse to ride or plow or pull,
Helped another neighbor shod a horse,
Sharpen his machetes or plow blade.

Their arms did not embrace,
They clothed us, healed and fed us.
Admonished us to carry our own weight
In home and community,
Disciplined, with stern looks,
Love and fear of God,
Mild spankings and *pellizcos*.
God given talents
Shared with family, neighbor, stranger.
Answered midnight knock
To pray for and aid a sick neighbor.
Read a Bible verse to console and uplift.

Their lips did not kiss,
They spoke only of the good in others.
Told us to be polite to friend and foe.
They blessed, encouraged, and taught
Their children and the whole village,
Read the news on the war,
To parents, spouses, siblings listening.
Led us in the ways of the Lord,
Shaped by the actions of love.

Sheltered By Love

Childhood memories
Spring forward in sharp focus
To invade and try to derail me.
Now I see what my heart felt
When I heard words my mind did not believe.
And understand the sadness in the pretty picture.

Now I hear words they did not say,
Understand their distractedness
For what is, but should not be.
Anxious to protect and shelter me
Let me be a child, innocent and unburdened,
While they dealt with illnesses and disappointments.

Now I see how my parents' spirit
Was dragged down by hard
Back-breaking labor, and
Harsh treatment in the outside world.
Service or entrance denied
"We do not serve dogs here."

With hindsight I realize
The enormous sacrifices
They and older siblings made
To spare me the same and
Even dislocate to larger city
To provide better opportunities.

At last I see how you learn
To let them hide their pain and doubts,
And you deal with your own.
Hide your own understanding.
To lighten parents' burdens.
Sheltered by love.

The Doorway To Aunt Hood

A quilt covered the doorway to the end room on that April morning in 1945. After breakfast, Mama told me to go out and play, but I'd heard the muffled voices behind the quilt, of *Tia* Pazita and *Comadre* Benita with my mother and my older sister. Doña Senona came in later and pinching my cheeks, said, "*Yo te traje a ti y tus hermanos al mundo.*" If she had brought us into the world, was she bringing a baby today? I certainly wanted to stick around. *Where did she bring them from?* I thought. No one was paying attention to me. *I could peek in.* I think *Diosito* knew I was not ready for that much knowledge because I just sat on the floor outside the room.

The women came out and back in with hot water, basins and sheets, and even doll clothes. Each time they told me to go out and play. My sister's loud moans and angry words broke the quiet and startled me. It seemed to me she was doing it more often and she got louder and angrier. Finally, I heard a lot of movement and Doña Senona saying, "*Ya, ya, empuja fuerte.*" And then a full throated baby cry! And I heard more movements. Then Doña Senona announced, "*Es un hombrecito.*"

Mama said, "*Que bueno que no es otra hembra para sufrir en este mundo.*"

So the baby was a boy and Mama was happy that it was not another female destined to suffer. But where had Doña Senona brought him from?? Why was my sister angry? I knew I was now an aunt, because my friend became an aunt when her older sister had a baby. I saw water flowing out from under the quilt and went to get old newspapers and a mop and I started cleaning. When Mama came out, I said proudly "*Ma Tia 'ta tapiando.*" She laughed and told the women the "little aunt is mopping". She came out again and showed me the most beautiful baby I had ever seen, dressed in the doll clothes: my oldest nephew Ignacio, whom I called Nachito, then later, Nash when he grew up. I would play with him, then look after him and take care of him off and on for the next sixty years.

I was not quite 5 years old, yet I felt that I needed to take care of him and, two years later, of his brother Eddie. I defended them, from older bullies in school. I made sure they wore shoes to protect their feet from the heat and thorns. I misinformed them about the birds and the bees, but I also taught them Spanish and English, helped them with their homework when they started school. Eddie liked to take his clothes off when we played in the sun and my sister would punish him. So I would pick up his clothes and carry them until we went in to eat. I would get him dressed before we did.

Because my sister lived with us with my two nephews, my parents had the same rules and expectations for the three of us: to "carry your own weight in the family" that they had taught me. My nephews grew up with the same anchors of faith, values and family unity, getting an education, helping others at home and in the community that I did.

When Nash and Eddie were nine and six my sister moved to Corpus Christi with them to get back together with their father. I missed them dearly, but we moved to Corpus two years later. When I saw boys and girls smoking and hanging around street corners, the boys dressed in black, with chains hanging from their pockets, their hair slicked back with Three Roses brilliantine, it really freaked me out. My nephews would not grow up like that. I signed them up at the Boys Club close to my house where they spent most afternoons and weekends.

My sister had her hands full, in a second marriage, taking care of two stepdaughters, holding down a full time job and selling Avon and Sara Coventry on the side. I felt I needed to provide stability and direction for Nash and Eddie. My brothers would drop the three of us at the movies, or they would go to the beach with us. When I got a car after I graduated from Nursing School, and waited out a semester until I moved to San Antonio to Incarnate Word University (IWU) to get my BS in Nursing, I took them and my other nieces and nephews to the beach, to play wee-tee golf, to the movies and the sock hops on the T-heads.

After IWU, I worked with the American Red Cross for one year and returned to Corpus. After Nash graduated from high school, I got him in as an Orthopedic Technician (OT) trainee at the hospital where I was training auxiliary personnel and helped him pay his tuition for college. When he joined the Navy, his training as an OT got him assigned as a Paramedic. He served in a hospital ship in Guam that received evacuated wounded soldiers from Vietnam. Eddie graduated from High School and went to Houston to study Political Science and work.

Nash came to live with me and my husband for a year in Puerto Rico (PR) after he was discharged from the Navy. He worked with my husband in electronics, and in the evenings he and I would talk about old times and his future. I sensed he needed time to decompress from the horrendous experience of treating young men who lost their limbs and more in service to their country. He told me that sometimes he had to perform minor surgical procedures while the surgeons were taking care of the wounded. My sister resented that he had not come directly home to her, but had come to live with me. He stayed with us about two years.

He decided to attend Nursing School in Houston where he joined Eddie. They bought a house together and took in roommates. As a nurse Nash scrubbed in with Dr. DeBakey and Dr. Cooley on heart transplants and cardiovascular surgeries. Eddie became an activist, helping immigrants get their citizenship and learn English as a second language. They started a Centro Aztlan that provided a broad range of services to immigrants and refugees, from legal to recreational services. My son went several summers to help at the Center, especially in the recreational services.

Nash, Eddie and I only saw each other when I came to spend the Christmas Holidays with family. It seemed that we were growing apart. They were getting different degrees, but both were actively involved with migrants and refugees, the Cesar Chavez labor movement, and protests, and finally became founding members of La Raza Unida Party. They were arrested multiple times for promoting civil unrest with their protests. I supported their social justice causes, helped them pay the rent, but could not embrace the "new Chicano nation" concept. I boycott lettuce in PR, in support of the movement.

When I moved back to Texas in 1978, they introduced me to political rallies, boycotts, protest marches, and eating at barrio restaurants with their Raza Unida friends. I realized I was of another generation and to them, I was part of the "establishment, management, upwardly mobile". We had accomplished my parents' dream: we'd gotten out of "coton azul", blue denim associated with hard labor and the cotton fields. Ideologically we were not that far apart, standing for social justice, equal opportunities for all. We had heated discussions about who was helping "la raza" more.

It upset me that they did not appreciate that being in management, I set policies for equal employment opportunities, pay and benefits, and ensured that "las razas" (all races) were treated with equal justice. I could never join their protests, because I had a phobia of police and guns. It developed as a child when "La Migra" rounded people up in the fields, refused to let my mother show our birth certificates. Once even my father, a six generation American was sent to Mexico. So we were different people acting in the public arena, but at the kitchen table were still family.

When Nash got married, he left nursing to become a lawyer at his wife's insistence. I baptized his middle son Stephen. Later he also left the Catholic faith and he converted to his wife's religion and stopped associating with our family for decades. Most of our family gatherings were in celebration of birthdays, Catholic milestones, Easter and Christmas holidays, all of which were banned in his new religion. At first, I understood that he would put family first and wanted to maintain peace and unity in his family. But I stopped reading his letters, when they became more and more evangelical anti-Catholic missives and less caring nephew and aunt communications.

In reality, as much as I loved them, when I left my husband, I moved back to Corpus, not to Houston. I went into survival mode. I visited Nash and Eddie in Houston as an outing for me and my kids, but I could not do it often. With two children to support, I'd had to start over career wise, under employed and underpaid. I was trying to go on with life as a mother, working as a Nurse Recruiter which entailed travel, getting a degree in Business Management more suited to the direction my career was taking.

God was opening doors for me and my career took off in Human Resources. I left the hospital environment when I got selected as Director of Professional and Minority Recruitment with the City of Corpus Christi (CC), then Director of HR for the newly formed CC Rapid Transit Authority. At the same time, it was very important to me to get myself and the kids involved in a parish. I volunteered to do the books for the parish Religious Education program in lieu of tuition for my two children. I also wanted my children to get to know my parents and their cousins so we visited often. I got a pass to State and National

Parks and we camped out a lot, sometimes taking one or two of their cousins. Fortunately the kids enjoyed that.

In 1990 I accepted a position as Manager of Recruitment and Employment with the Dallas Area Rapid Transit, leaving my 22 year old son at home to continue his studies. My daughter was already in San Antonio working and studying at the University of Texas – San Antonio (UTSA). I needed the higher salary to help them through school. It came with more responsibility, as well as more opportunities. In six months, my boss was fired, and I was named Acting Director of HR and then selected as the Director. Five men had held that position in five years. I held it until I retired in 2001 as Assistant Vice President-Human Resources and settled in San Antonio to be an active grand-mother to my grandson.

In November 2003, Nash was admitted to the VA Hospital in San Antonio, near death. Steroids, prescribed for a persistent pneumonia ten or twelve years before, had shut down his immune system, causing skin cancers and multiple system breakdowns. He had struggled for years to wean himself off, but this wonder drug would destroy him. My oldest sister Carmen and I visited him almost daily, bringing him bean and cheese tacos and *Calabaza con pollo y elote,* which he loved. I supplied him with glyconutrients which were proving effective in boosting the immune system.

He talked proudly of working with Dr. DeBakey, calling it his dream job. I concluded that Nash was obliterating himself, first by giving up his faith and nursing, which resulted in alienation from family and finally, by his dependence on steroids and pain medications.

When he was discharged after nine months, he was off the steroids and cancer free. He seemed to thrive and was trying to be the husband and father he'd always wanted to be. I continue to supply the glyco-nutrients until he restarted his law practice again and began to order them himself.

When his wife and kids had visited Nash at the VA Hospital, they stayed with me and we got close. Early in July Vanessa, his oldest daughter, and her two roommates spent the weekend with me for a fun time in San Antonio. I was happy to have them. Sadly, on July 23, 2004, Vanessa and her two friends were killed in a terrible car accident. Stephen her brother was in the car also, but thank God he was only slightly injured. At 17, he cradled his sister in his arms until she died in the ER.

This was a big setback for Nash and once again, he began taking the steroids and pain killers, and he stopped taking the supplements. In early March 2005, we had our last conversation. Nash passed away late March, just before his sixtieth birthday. Stephen had to be the one to find his dad, when he came home between his two part time jobs in the middle of the night. My brother Rene and I wanted to pray over him before they cremated his body. We explained to his half-brother who belonged to Jehovah's Witnesses that Nash was a baptized Catholic and we wanted to commend his soul to Jesus in our own way. He spoke to the elders, and finally he called me. "Our hearts are with you and Rene, and we know how much you loved him. We have arranged a room for you and we will have his body in a casket. Please remember that the body can only be out for twenty minutes. Also, his face... " I did not let him finish. "Nash and I spoke about his wishes. He did not want a viewing." He seemed relieved. Rene and Mary, Eddie and I prayed together and left Eddie alone with his brother the last few minutes. That was the last thing I did for Nash.

My relationship with my nephews is part of my journey of faith and they were a part of my formative years. They really rescued me from being raised as an only child. Because I was older my parents expected me to set a good example for them. I hear my mother saying, *"La familia es sagrada."* The sacred bonds of family, lead us to fill a need, move into any role called for. I am struck with the irony of my mother's words when Nash was born: *"Que bueno que no es otra hembra para sufrir en este mundo."* In her world, women were born to suffer, not just in childbirth. They sacrificed their own aspirations to follow their men and mother their children. They had to be submissive to their husbands, who had all the power and freedom.

My nephew did suffer and sacrifice, but faced life with a brave determination and ambition. He was a successful nurse and then a lawyer. Writing this has helped me to grieve his death and Vanessa's. I even admit to myself that Nash made some bad decisions, but this does not change my love for him. I know I was there for him till the end.

Eddie and his children continue to be a big part of my family and I am proud that he continues to be an advocate for refugees and immigrants, hands on and even as part of a subcommittee in the United Nations for that program. He founded the South Texas Human Rights Center, which is a central point for information and services to migrants and their families. He personally puts water stations in the brush country with written permission from landowners, forms coalitions with law enforcement agencies for search and rescue for lost migrants. He ensures that DNA testing is done on bodies found, inventory articles found with or near the body, which might help identify the body for families. It is also a center for other organizations such as forensic groups who look for unmarked graves all over border communities, exhume the bodies to do DNA testing that is paired with the grave marking, maintain a database and phone line to help families find lost ones. They provide decent burial, with the family present when possible. My son and I support him in various concrete ways and moral support. At my church people let me know that they saw Eddie on TV and let their friends proudly know that I am the aunt of Eddie Canales.

Funny how once again at 80 and 73, Eddie and I are of the same generation, but still politically disparate. Someday we will all be in a place where there is no suffering, no religious or political differences, only The One Truth.

Reflection:

1. Has my family espoused causes or religious traditions that carry on from one generation to another?

2. Has my family learned to accept different ideologies, faith traditions and lifestyles while still maintaining that family ties are sacred?

3. How does my family support family members and their causes in their efforts, even if we don't necessarily embrace the cause?

2

FAMILY, FAITH AND TRADITIONS

Christmas Angel

Our very own Santa Claus came from Cuero, Texas to Saliñeno mid-November, bearing sacks of pecans, apples, oranges, ribbon candy and the biggest peppermint sticks ever. Tío Salvador, my favorite uncle, his eyes crinkling and belly shaking, had a wheezing hee-hee-hee laugh that started deep in his gut. I feared that he was not getting enough air and he'd faint. Reassuringly, he'd scoop me up on his knee. For several days he filled our lives with his contagious laugh, jokes and pranks. Before he left, Tío dumped a sack of pecans from an oak tree as we gleefully dodged them below. He wanted us to have the experience of picking pecans. It was curious to see Mama, not as a mom, but almost like a kid playing and joking with her older brother.

He was a real cowboy: tall and lanky, bowlegged. He wore faded jeans, scuffed boots, chaps and a wide brimmed Panama hat with sides bent down in front and back. His skin was leathered and tanned by hard work in the sun, wind and rain on the ranch he managed all his adult life. He did not carry a gun but had a sheathed knife on his hip and a rifle handy for rattlesnakes, deer hunting and shooting bull frogs in the cattle watering hole.

He was well known in Cuero, Yoakum and Sheepside for his integrity and willingness to help those in need. He organized fundraisers for families in need or for a community hit by a natural disaster. Tío Salvador's presence loomed bigger than life with love and respect from family, friends and business acquaintances.

He held an annual birthday party on Labor Day weekend to celebrate his, his wife's and daughter's, my dad's and my birthday. There was lots of food, music and visiting with my grandmother and family from all over. I counted mobile homes with license plates from eight different states hooked up on the grounds.

The highlight of the weekend for kids was to pile into his jeep to run an errand in town. As scary as riding with him was, we never turned him down. He told jokes the whole time, turning back to look at us in the back seat, laughing. Oh, and he drove in the middle of the road!!! It was uncanny how he adjusted to his side of the road and quit talking when a car approached.

The last party I remember attending was in 1958 when I had just started nursing school the week before. He grabbed me by the hand and proudly introduced me as "the future family nurse". He also proudly introduced my cousin Phil Ramon, in his uniform! Tío had driven to Lackland Airforce Base in San Antonio to pick him up for the party, asked to talk to the Base Commander, whom he informed that he was there to pick up Phil for the weekend. He explained that this was a perfect opportunity for Phil, who grew up in Michigan, to meet family from Texas and all over.

Phil was not the only one surprised when the Commander granted him a three-day pass, sent an officer to inform his Drill Sergeant, and together they informed Phil at his barracks, that "someone" needed to see him. When he came out, he saw our uncle, whom he had not seen since he was seven. The Sergeant asked Phil, "Do you know this man? He showed up to pick you up." Luckily Phil remembered Tío from a picture he had seen in his home for years. All he said was, *"Tío."* Sometimes not knowing how things are supposed to work is best.

When my parents and I moved to Corpus Christi in 1955, Tío visited us more often, but he no longer brought goodies for a whole village. He did bring venison, and sweaters crocheted by Tia Agustina and cousin Criselia.

Update: When I retired in San Antonio, TX, in 2001, one Sunday after Mass, I stopped the Cantor to compliment her voice. After a few minutes, she said, "Belza, I'm sorry, I have to go, my family is waiting for me. We're going to Yoakum to see family."

I said, "Really? I used to go to a ranch near Yoakum when I was growing up, to see my grandmother and uncle. He had a birthday party every year on Labor Day weekend and lots of family came from all over."

She said in surprise, "Really! Salvador Vera?? We used to go almost every year. I wonder if we are related."

We became good friends, but never found out if we were related. In 2019 I attended her funeral services and sought out her family to offer my condolences. I related how we had learned we'd probably been at Tío Salvador's annual party together years before. Her youngest sister said, "Really!! He and his wife Agustina are my Baptismal Godparents!! They are probably Godparents to half the county." I believe that.

White Christmas in South Texas*

Our house seemed so quiet after Tío Salvador left, until we started preparations for Christmas. We shelled pecans for the stuffing, candies, *pan de polvo*, and pies that Mama made, our house filling with mouthwatering aromas, tempting us to sneak a taste. A few days before Christmas, Papa put a package of small paper sacks and the goodies that Tío Salvador had brought on the large kitchen table. He expertly sliced each peppermint stick into one and a half-inch rounds and the ribbon candy into sections with a hack saw.

"What are you doing, Papa?" I asked.

"Did you think all this candy was for you?"

"Of course not, I was planning on sharing it with Eddie and Nash."

"Come, help me wrap up the candy and fill up these sacks. Write the name of each kid in your class on a bag and put one piece of each type of candy, one fruit and some pecans in each one. Make one for you cousins too."

"Papa, my grade is divided into three groups: A, B, and C according to how smart we are. I'm in the A group, so that's my class."

"Start with the C's and see if we have enough for the A's."

That kept me honest. Mama joined us to help. In the evening, inspired by the Sears Catalog's offerings of Currier and Ives Christmas cards, we colored loose leaf paper to make chain link garlands and made flocking. Mama brought out snowflakes, angels, candles and ice-skates that she had tatted or knit, which we dipped in the flocking mix, with Dreft Soap flakes, liquid starch, flour and water, and set them out to dry.

In 90° F weather in South Texas, we transformed our frame home by the Rio Grande into a Currier and Ives Christmas scene. We cut out all the figures for the Nativity from the catalog, backed them with cardboard and placed them in the crèche Papa had made long ago. Or we would just repair any that had suffered in storage from last year.

As we worked Mama told us the story of the birth of Jesus. If a rare Texas Norther blew in, Papa fed logs into the *chimenea* to keep us warm. Memories of working with my older brothers, made me a bit sad. My parents missed them too so we told stories about their pranks, like Rene wetting a piece of string with saliva and wrapping it around the glass on the lit kerosene lamp. Clink, total darkness, to the shed for a spanking. My older sister, Carmen and Connie, left home by the time I was two so I barely remembered them. But when Connie lived with us with my two nephews Nash and Eddie, they too helped make decorations.

A week before Christmas we cut a mesquite or willow branch for our tree and stuck it into a can full of dirt. We made more flocking for the tree and to accumulate as "snow" outside on the window sills, the edge of the roof and front stoop.

We topped the tree with a big star, covered with foil gum wrappers. We wrapped **empty** gift boxes to put under it. If times were good, my mother ordered new clothes and shoes from the Sears Catalog, made a new outfit for me from flour cloth sacks that she collected until there was enough cloth for a dress. But of course we wore our new outfits to Christmas Mass. We did not have real presents under the tree.

Even though my son and daughter and my grandchildren do not worship together with me, we celebrate Christmas, Easter and secular holidays together. We maintain awareness of the Christian significance of Holy Days while still allow Santa and the Easter Bunny to have their day as long as the children believe in them.

My Family at Christmas 2009

*(I read this story on Texas Public Radio, Texas Matters Program, one year, and they re-aired it for several years, just before Christmas.)

Midnight Mass

Midnight Mass used to actually start at midnight. It was fun staying up for *Misa de Gallo*. By 11:30 PM we walked over to Church to see the live Nativity scene, with children picked by my mother as recognition for progress with their prayers, standing around the *pesebre* my father made. Baby Jesus was the newest resident in the village that the manger would still hold. My mother got the altar ready for the visiting priest. After Mass, people and the priest came to our house, for the blessed Baby Jesus, a swaddled doll, put in the manger before we left and a *desayuno* of yeast bread and *chocolate con canela*.

At dawn, parents walked home with sleepy kids carrying the brown paper sacks full of goodies, thanks to Tío Salvador. Papa and Mama let me do the honors of distributing the bags to my classmates. Yes, there had been enough goodies for A, B, and C's, my nephews and I, and even for my cousins. I let everyone know that MY Tío Salvador was the real Santa Claus who had brought the goodies all the way from Cuero, Texas.

Later we would have our Christmas meal: a roasted chicken, stuffed with corn bread dressing. Of course, we had our quintessential *tamales* made with venison and pork, and pumpkin *empanadas*. I bet we could teach Currier and Ives a thing or two about tamales for Christmas. Homemade desserts were served with hot chocolate.

The Magi, (actual store bought figurines) who started their journey from the back door in mid-December, moved closer to the Nativity each day, arriving by January 6 (Three Kings Day), to adore Jesus. We all knelt in adoration, as Mama told us about Herod ordering the killing of all two-year old baby boys. An angel told Joseph to take Mary and Jesus to Egypt to hide until it was safe to return to Nazareth.

Cleanup day was hard, getting all that "snow" off took a lot of scrubbing. For me, the family preparing and sharing a meal, celebrating the Birth of Jesus at Midnight Mass, even cleaning up, and storing my Nativity Figurines in their Styrofoam molds to store, is still the essence of Christmas.

Easter Reflections

John 14: 1-12 *e. I will come back again and take you to myself, so that where I am you also may b*e.

John 19: 16-18. *So they took Jesus, and carrying the cross himself, went out to what is called the Place of the Skull, in Hebrew, Golgotha. There they crucified him, and with him two others, one on either side, with Jesus in the middle.*

The Scripture narratives for Easter and the crucifixion are so painful for me to read and reflect on. As a child, since my mother was the only Lector in my small town, I would ask her "Please, this year can you tell a happier ending to the story." It was even more painful when I finally understood it was not a story and the ending could not be changed. Jesus had to die for our sins.

But oh, the Resurrection narrative brings joy and hope. Jesus promises me that he has a place for me and he wants me there. I will not get there through some magical thinking. I will not get there unless I live every day mindfully with all its challenges. But I had to make a decision at some point that Jesus is my Lord and Savior, that I believe there is life everlasting and that I want to follow Jesus.

When the challenges seem hard or seem to come at me as fast and hurtful as hail, I just need to remember: Jesus is waiting for me to present me to His Father. **I must be ready.**

(Shared via SKYPE with my Global Small Christian Community, St. Isidore of Seville)

My Human Heart Cannot Bear

What human heart is not touched
That a sinless loving man
Was publicly humiliated and scourged?
That we would do this to your Son,
Oh Lord, my heart is shamed.

What mother's heart can remain cold
That Mary witnessed every insult
Suffered on Her Son
On the road to Calvary?
Oh Lord, my heart is broken.

What heart can forget
That a father gave his only son
To die for us because he loved us,
His other children?
Oh Lord, let my heart be grateful.

What heart does not burn
With the joy of resurrection?
Triumph over death once and for all.
That we may live in your eternal glory.
But Oh Lord, let my heart yearn for it.

What heart can hold on
To this great gift,
And keep from sharing it,
With fallen brother, fallen sister
Living in frozen tundra?

Oh Lord, let me open my heart.
Extend an open hand,
Speak of your love and mercy
And bring them home
To warm and welcoming hearth.

Stay With Us – Witness In Faith

Preparing for Lent takes a lot of preparation! I decide and plan for an act of mercy to embrace for forty days. This year I am going to donate a food a day to St. Vincent de Paul Center and actually do the daily reflections in the little black book. Also, I block out the days for the Easter services that I will be a Lector for. The Coordinator assigns us in the order that he gets our requests so I let him know my availability way ahead of the special services of Easter week, with a reminder that this will be my nteenth year to read at the Tenebrae and the Seven Last Words of Christ services, my favorites. I study the readings assigned to me. My own SCC visited Seven Churches on Holy Thursday for years, so I would clean out my car, specially the trunk, for the wheel chair and couple of walkers that had to go in and out, in and out seven times. Is it a sacrifice if you actually enjoy doing something?

I start preparing for the secular celebration of Easter also, as my mother did ever since I can remember. The Resurrection is a cause for joy, after all. For a couple of months before Lent I start making *cascarones:* saving the empty egg shells with a hole at the pointy end. Umm, come to think of it we eat more omelets and breakfast tacos during Easter. I get Easter baskets for my grandkids, girly things to put in two of them and boy things for the third. (*Not too much candy, Mom*, I hear my daughter saying.) I buy the things needed to finish the *cascarones,* food coloring, and confetti to fill them with, tissue to seal the hole, glue, and plastic grass for the bunnies in the baskets.

Our Easter picnic has been at my son's lake house, on Lake Corpus Christi several times. Memories of past Easter picnics bring joy: on the dry creek beds on the Rio Grande River as a child, a beach or river park in Corpus as a teenager, a *pachanga and lechon asao'* with friends in the 13 years we lived in Puerto Rico. Always and everywhere we practice the same barbaric ritual of breaking all those *cascarones* on each other's heads. Some people get so creative with the filling.

During Lent I will also do my Easter contact calls, because my mother used to send out cards to those friends and family whom you love but are not in frequent contact with. Some years the call is also an act of mercy, for I reach people at a time of need for consolation, encouragement, prayer or healing.

Then come the beautiful, moving celebrations of the Triduum, Easter Vigil with the washing of the feet, the RCIA receiving their Sacraments, and glorious Easter Sunday. It sorrows me that my family does not worship with me, but I am surrounded by my SCC brothers and sisters in Christ. We gather in the Narthex after services for hugs from their kids and fellowship. I love that I get to see them grow to teenagers and young adults.

Christ has died, Christ is risen and He will come again!! The disciples on the road to Emmaus, did not know this, but we do. They were returning to their old life, downtrodden and sad, having lost their leader, their hope for a liberating Messiah. Then a sojourner like them joins them, Jesus, but they did not recognize him. He made sense of the events of the last few days with familiar scriptures from the Old Testament. He witnessed in faith to them, giving comfort and understanding.

Stay with us, they said to him, as darkness came. Were they speaking from their need to stave off the darkness of hopelessness? Or were they speaking from genuine concern for this stranger traveling alone in the dark of night? Stay with us, for you give us hope. So he stayed with them for the best was yet to come in the breaking of the bread at supper. They recognize Jesus! This was the right moment – with understanding and a hopeful heart they could really see Him. Their hearts were burning and they acted, they returned to Jerusalem to share their hope and witness to their brothers and sisters.

I want to say: Christ stay with me, with us a while longer. I want to experience my heart burning. I want to respond like the two disciples did. I want to walk with you and share my hope with others. Should I be asking Him to help me to stay with Him, instead? To make my heart burn with desire to build His Kingdom on earth, in my own heart and life?

For Reflection:

1.   When have I failed to recognize or listen to Jesus?

2.   When has someone walked with me on my journey, explaining scripture to me and set my heart burning?

3.   Have I done that for others?

Two Months for Mary

May is the Month of Mary and October is the Month of the Rosary. San Jose Church was one of the first community structures erected in Salineño (founded as Rancho Salinas), on the round boulder by the river that is still there. Our families took on the legacy to maintain the church and clean it since it was on land donated by our great grandparents. There was and still is no priest assigned there. San Jose is a mission church in the Archdiocese of Brownsville. TX.

It was my Mother who made it "Church" throughout the liturgical year. She was the catechist who prepared generations of children for their sacraments, and even prepared parents and godparents for their children's Baptism, couples before marriage and every child for such important milestones. She gathered people in the church to pray novenas for the soul of persons who passed away, for the end of the war, for healing during some epidemics.

She celebrated the Month of Mary (May) and the Month of the Rosary (October) with daily Rosaries in Spanish followed by the Litany of Loretto. The children and youth processed in singing *Ave, Ave Maria,* with fresh flowers from their gardens for Mary.

Regardless of what language is used to recite the Rosary, I always hear it and the litany in Spanish and in Mama's voice.

Dios Padre del Cielo, ten piedad de nosotros.

Madre De Dios, Ruega por nosotros

Madre purísima, Madre de la Divina Gracia, Virgen más poderosa, Torre de David, Torre de Marfil, Ruega por nosotros.

Her devotion to Mary was evident in our modest home with a niche in every room and a statue or framed picture of Mary and a votive candle. A hollow statue of Our Lady of Guadalupe in one, a mirror frame with the Sacred Hearts of Jesus and Mary in another. Fatima and Lourdes in the other rooms. A small plaster icon of Our Lady of Perpetual Help leaning in another. Its edges worn down by years of Mama's hands holding it. A crucifix was also hung over the doorway of every room, and entrances.

Papa told me once that he always knew when Mama was expecting a baby, because she would buy a new statue of Mary and a Crucifix and then say, "Antonio, bring Matilde (his brother) so I –we – can tell him where to build a new room".

First Communion in Community

My mother chose me to carry on our family responsibility, because as soon as I made my First Communion she made me her assistant. After we moved, my cousin continued with it.

Maybe I took that responsibility much too seriously. There was one little girl, two or three years younger than I, that did not pay attention, jumping around and talking. After several admonitions from my mother she kept on doing it. I went to her and grabbed her arm firmly, and pulled her down to sit, whispering strongly "Sit down and keep quiet. You're in church."

She wailed loudly, "*Ay, me trozas mi brazito.*" She said I was breaking her little arm! I had nightmares for several nights, where her forearm ended in my hands.

One Easter Mass, when I lined up all the Communicants to process in, one girl fainted. When the priest started incensing the Altar, my cousin Jisa and another girl fainted, and a boy looked really ashen. Somehow I thought that was my fault also. Another year when the same thing happened with an adult, I told Mama, "Now, I am not taking responsibility for that. " She laughed and said, "It's the combination of gardenia and incense, plus the heat. It's too much for some. You are not to blame."

We were involved beyond the three or four months of preparation because one or two families left their children with us when they went "al West or al Norte" to pick cotton or harvest other crops, so that the children would make their 1ˢᵗ Communion or Confirmation with their peers. It was kind of fun because we shared the big room at our home, since all my older siblings were gone. We did our homework together and if they needed help learning their prayers we took time to practice. We said our morning and evening prayers together. I had playmates when I roamed in the brush. My cousin Jisa and I reminisce about that. Several weeks before Easter, Mama made the girls' veils and even dresses for some. She also cut some of the boys' hair and made black bow ties for them.

After Easter Mass, we gathered at our house, under the sparse trees for the traditional *desayuno*. Since the custom back then was fasting since midnight to receive the Eucharist, there was a hearty breakfast and sweet homemade bread, *pan de polvo* and chocolate.

This was a community celebration and everyone contributed whatever they could. Some brought extra tables, chairs and tablecloths the night before. Others came early before Mass to set up. All the women served. The priest was always invited and usually came, unless he had to drive to another little town for a later Mass.

This was not only a unifying event for our village, but an opportunity to invite more people to come to church regularly. Even if some families did not come to church on Sundays, most had their children baptized and make 1st Communion and Confirmation.

Mama and I on my 1st Communion

3

SQUARE PEG FITS IN A CIRCLE – WITH HELP FROM A FEW ANGELS

What's In a Name?

On my birth certificate, my name is spelled with an 's', Belsa, probably because my father registered us months after we were bornand he forgot Mama's instructions. Several of us had to file for a correction, when we married, or filed for Social Security. On my Baptismal certificate and school records though, filled out in my mother's hand writing, my name is spelled with a "z". I like Belza better so I too asked for a corrected copy. I always thought my mother had made up my name, and there were no other Belza's.

Some years ago, the Minister of Cultural Affairs of Spain, came to Corpus Christi to confer the Order of Isabela, the Catholic on Dr. Cleo Garcia for founding the Spanish American Genealogical Society at a big banquet. Because I worked for the City, I bought a table for my family and my name was on a banner in the center. The Minister walked around chatting at every table and read my name. He said "That's a Basque name, very popular in Spain." He said it means "full bodied and robust, like good wine". It describes me perfectly and it amazes me that I have lived up to it, without realizing its meaning.

The Spanish origin of my name was again confirmed more recently when I travelled to Spain. As the young man at the Money Exchange gave me Euros for US dollars, he made a copy of my passport face page. He asked,

"How come you have an American passport?"

I replied, "Because I am American – seventh generation."

"Not with a name like "Belza" he retorted. "That is a very well-known, old Spanish name."

Knowing that, makes me feel rooted in my ancestral heritage, and in the traditions, faith, language and cuisine that is so much a part of my upbringing. It's solid ground beneath my feet, a tapestry woven from traces of DNA, textured and patterned by experiences in my life, given depth by Christ in me, like brocade. If viewed at an angle it assumes different depths. To truly see who I am, you must look straight and long.

Life on the Margin

As our mothers washed quilts on the big rocks on the banks of El Rio Grande, we kids played in the water close to the edge. One of my favorite pastimes was to pitch dry mud planks low over the water surface, so that they went a-skippin and a-jumpin. I wanted them to reach the other *frontera* but that only happened when the river dried down to its deepest middle.

What made the clay mud dry up in almost perfect squares with the corners curled up? Why would they sink if you tossed them in the direction of the current and skip on the surface if you tossed them against or across the current? Why did some of the kids never catch on to that?

If there were kids "*allá, al otro lado*", they tossed mud planks our way and we yelled insults at each other *en español*. Shouldn't a common language, music, food bind us together? Their last names were like ours, but I bet their teachers didn't mispronounce them like ours did. I bet they weren't punished for speaking *español*.

I asked Mama these questions once and the women raised their heads and stared at me and Mama seemed embarrassed,

"*¿Esta muchacha, de dónde saca esas cosas?*" If I asked Papa, he would disown me. "*¿De dónde saca **TU HIJA** esas cosas?*" he asked Mama. Once he told me,

"*Vas a sufrir mucho en esta vida*, because you think like a man." He walked away when I asked,

"*Pues,* how come men don't suffer for thinking like men? I only know one way to think."

Natural Preserve for Exotic Birds and Plants

Me Sitting on the Founding Rock

RGRiver Swimming Area

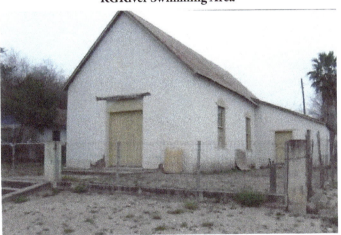

San Jose Church in Salineño

Fronteras– Spider Webs in My Mind

All kinds of people came to and through our *frontera*. It broke up the monotony of our lives, but the grown-ups were wary they would give the young people "ideas" and they would want to leave. So we were not allowed to interact with them. I was very curious about them. Where did they come from, how did they find our village, where did the stuff they sold come from. I especially wanted to know in what way they were different.

There were the colorful "Húngaros", the band of gypsies who came in the winter and parked their covered trucks in the plaza. They were fortune tellers, sold potions for every illness or to make someone love or desire you more. They sold bright clothes and bead jewelry, door to door. At night though, clothes hung out on the clotheslines, flower pots, swings, even the heavy iron *pailas*, used to gather rain water, anything not rooted to the ground, would disappear. The trucks and everything were gone in the morning.

Comanche Indians came to harvest the *peyote* for their "religious rites" from the fields. My blond, blue-eyed grandfather and his cousin were abducted by the Comanche as adolescents, during one of those forays around 1870. They escaped five or six years later. No other child had been taken since, but the fear endured and we were kept indoors until the Indians left.

Gringos (I thought it was "green grows") drove off State Highway 83, and went to the river to fish for alligator gar, catfish, and white bass. My brother says he'd follow them when they drove past the arroyo, to practice his English with them and learn about using different baits.

There were los *barrileros, Mejicanos*, who came at night at appointed times, with fresh meat, *piloncillo* and *tequila* floated across the river in wooden barrels. One night, I saw Papa selecting cuts of meat on the kitchen table. He'd already set bottles of tequila, El Presidente brandy, Bacardi rum and *piloncillos* out on the counter. A wet stranger looked silently on. Both ignored me and when I questioned Papa the next day, he said

"*Estabas soñando.*" walking away. But there was meat in the ice chest, so I knew it was not a dream. Why was it okay for this wet stranger to come into our home in the middle of the night while we slept yet I could not talk to him?

Then there were *Mejicanos,* working in the *Unaitis,* sneaking back to México for a visit. They got off the bus on Highway 83 and walked the two miles to our village to rendezvous with relatives at the river, who would cross them back to Mexico. One night we were sitting on the stoop, listening to my grandmother's ghost stories. Two men dressed in black and wearing black hats, walked toward our house across the empty lot in front of us. I thought it was my brothers who were living in Chicago and wrote about how the gangsters dressed like that. *They were coming to visit, and it was just like them to dress to impress the girls in our village.* I ran happily toward them and everyone started whispering loudly, "Belza, *no, no, dejalos pasar, vente."* The palpable fear in their voices, calling me back, was contagious and I froze. But the two men just got off the path away from me and with their faces turned away from me, went quietly by. They were more interested in not being seen. My mother ran toward me and grabbed me back to the stoop.

"Muchacha, cuantas veces te he dicho que es mejor ignorar la gente que pasa por la frontera." I started crying, my fear abating in her arms, but disappointed it was not my brothers.

Occasionally people came who were welcomed, like itinerant salesmen and photographers and even The Circus. They came in and paid the first curious kid they saw to distribute flyers ahead of them. That is why some of us have pictures sitting on a pony and I had a set of Encyclopedia Britannica and a First Communion picture.

I wonder now what the real "frontera" is. Is the web of fears planted in our minds the real *"frontera"*? The web of prejudices, of suspicion of anyone "who is not like us" creates an insurmountable barrier. Is a *"frontera"* a barrier to keep people out or a passage for people in search of a better life on the other side? Or are these people just making a living providing goods and experiences not found in the dusty small *frontera* towns?

Whenever I was confused or could not figure things out, I said I had cobwebs in my brain. It begins the day you are born *en la frontera,* fed to you in your mother's milk. Why do some venture out, try to get an education or learn a trade and others never do? Those who do leave, do the anxieties and fears in the big city hold us back? For certain, being timid makes you an open target for those who would take advantage of you. Are there people beyond our *fronteras,* who fear us?

Life after Midnight by the Radio

During the early morning hours in South Texas while it was still dark, I would turn the tuner slowly on the radio until I found an English station or "La Voz the America Latina", the volume low so as not to wake anybody.

I listened to *"Los Niños Catedráticos"*, super smart kids reciting poetry, reading essays or doing math calculations at the speed of a modern day computer. And I dreamed of joining them, but I had no idea how. The beauty of the Vienna Boys Choir made me cry. My favorite was listening to the Grand Ole' Opry. Those "somebody done somebody wrong" songs were not any different from our *corridos.* The two step rhythm just made me get up, dance and stomp around. That's what got me in trouble. The floor vibrations in our small frame home woke Mama and Papa. They sprang out of bed.

*"Que estas haciendo, muchacha? That's gringo music and I forbid you to listen to it. What's wrong with **your** daughter?"* Papa yelled at Mama. *"I tell you, she's going to bring big trouble to herself, getting all sorts of ideas from that music."*

Different?

Growing up, I just felt I didn't fit the mold people tried to put me in, not really feeling different. My parents loved me and were proud of me, but I realize now they feared that I would be hurt when I grew up. My brothers challenged me to recite lists (of Presidents, State Capitals, multiplication tables) as entertainment for them or their friends. My friends would have me look at a page and then ask me to "read it" back. Even my children would later test me when they were doing their homework when they came across something they thought "mom is not going to know this or remember this."

"Mom, where is Mesopotamia on the map?" "You need to get an old map, because it is now the Middle East mostly. Iran was Persia for a while. The two rivers from its meaning are the Tigris and Euphrates."

"Chucks, Mom." Someone lost a bet. Wish I could still do it!

They all feared that I would not be financially able or allowed to fulfill **my** dreams of being a nurse. They had experiences with people who viewed them as not worthy of entering a restaurant or getting a haircut because of their color or accent or last name when they were migrant workers. More so if someone tried to get ahead by going to a trade school or college. Hearing "we don't serve dogs here" set my father off one time and he almost ended up in jail. (On the other hand, the Ranger that escorted them out of the restaurant, asked that the truck follow him, with patrol car lights blazing. He took him to his ranch and fed them.) My parents were fifth and sixth generation American, and still had not attained equality. But hope is eternal.

I grew up at a time when children were supposed to be seen but not heard. It must have been hard for my parents to balance encouraging me but at the same time rein me in. They were protecting me from being too different. In raising us to fear and obey God they did teach me the humility to not offend or intimidate others. I remember one of my brothers always saying "that is not right or fair." He did not say "you're wrong" or "you are not being fair". My brothers were my idols so I imitated them. In everything.

Looking back I can see how my ways vexed adults, and made me a curiosity to my peers. I offered solutions to adult problems, or suggested more effective ways to do things. With a photographic memory and almost total recall I read everything: labels, the Sears catalog, my father's Agricultural leaflets, my textbooks, my older siblings' text books and corrected misquotes, even when it seemed to them that I was not engaged with their conversation. I still follow different conversations in the room.

I learned to read and write Spanish during a six week stay with two Spanish teachers who were Mama's nieces, when she had to have radiation therapy for a tumor in Laredo. I picked up English listening to my older brothers do their homework, all before I started school.

In our two room school house I learned 1st grade, and the other two grades being taught by one teacher. When I was done with my work, she would ask me to help others. This was not learning to pass a test. This was learning forever. I was skipped to third grade where I could also listen and learn 4th, 5th and 6th grade in the other room, if I sat close to the accordion door.

Though I could have been skipped again, my parents and teacher decided I needed to stay within my "maturity level". They explained why that was better for me. But they also said that it would embarrass older boys that I would pass up and embarrass their parents. They said something that I would later have to tell my son: that when you are very smart, someone will always try to bring you down. You need the maturity and humility to always bring others up so that they don't feel threatened.

That summer my parents did something that I know was a great sacrifice, perhaps to make it up to me and feed my need to learn more. It still moves me to remember it and see it as a God-incidence. An itinerant salesperson came to our village selling Encyclopedia Britannica sets that included beautiful leather bound tomes of the Classic writers like Shakespeare, Cyrano de Bergerac, Dickens, Mark Twain and others. They even continued to buy the annual updates for years. I read them all, and shared the encyclopedias with my classmates. That set went with me even to Puerto Rico when we moved with my husband's job.

I did not compete with others, though I did try to get to the Laredo Times crossword puzzle before my brother Rene did. He is 13 years older than I. He got even madder if I finished a puzzle he'd started. I competed with myself by improving the time it took me to do a task, or a game, like skip rope longer, faster, better than yesterday. That is not so-o odd, others did it too, but one day I pondered why I did everything with my right hand. It did not seem fair that my left hand was hardly used, so I gradually taught myself to write with my left hand, to iron my brothers' shirts, to wash dishes and to hang clothes with both hands. I started timing how long it took to do a task and try to "improve" the time each day. Until I started breaking dishes!

I didn't just climb trees, I did "exercises" similar to what my granddaughters call gymnastics, though I had never even heard the word. My father smoothed out several branches on the oak trees for me to walk on, jump, swing, turn, hang from my ankles, from my knees and do crunches, passing my feet between my hands and hang backwards. My brothers started calling me "*changa*" because I must have looked like a monkey, but I thought it was because I was ugly.

In Roma, in the 7th grade, my math teacher observed that I arrived at the correct math answers with steps different than she taught me and faster. I also spelled words in rhythms, beating my fingers on my thigh.

She asked me if I would like to compete in the State Interscholastic meets for math, spelling and debate. I did!! I had to do fifty calculations in one minute in my head, to qualify. My dream of being a Whiz Kid came true!

A few years ago, when I attended a 70th birthday celebration for my sister-in-law's sister in Los Saenz, which is annexed to Roma, family and friends that I had not seen in years, joyfully and (loudly) called my name when I arrived and as we hugged. A very thin and elderly lady, also called out, "Belza Ramos, I was your teacher in Salineño in 1949." I would have been in the fifth grade since I skipped 2nd grade. Naturally, as soon as I could, I sat down to talk to her. I asked her how come she remembered me. She said,

"You were a little Einstein."

I laughed, "How come I'm not famous like he is?" She said,

"Oh, you've done alright for yourself. People keep me posted." I thanked her for teaching me well.

None of this is remarkable, but in my journey of faith I realize that I did not give God credit for any of it. Though I also did not give myself credit for it, either, it was what it was. I wish I had made that most important connection much earlier than I did. But I thank God I did eventually.

Me with Maria Santos, my 4th Grade teacher in 1949

The Form Sent Me to the Principal's Office

In 1953 with the building of the Falcon Dam, the sudden injection of over 250 Anglo "Dam Kids" changed the dynamics of our school and the area. During the building of the dam, the locals were not being hired even for entry level jobs, until the League of United Latin American Citizens (LULAC) and the GI Forum got involved, organizing demonstrations and letter writing campaigns to Senators and Representatives.

More kids, more teachers, and more choices of extra-curricular clubs we could join. I chose "Other" on the form and wrote in "Health Club" on the blank line. A few days later I was called to the Principal's office.

"Explain what you mean by "Health Club. Why did you write that in?"

"Was that wrong?" I asked fearfully. But then I added, "Why would you have a blank that says 'Other', if you don't want it to be a choice?"

He had my file in front of him, and glancing down he asked, "Ramos, from Salineño. Are you as smart as your brothers?

"Smarter." I answered modestly. I had overheard my brothers tell my parents to stop following the crops, and to keep me in school all year, because "she's smarter than any of us." They said they would help them with money.

Half smiling, he said "Well, certainly more assertive. Nobody has **ever** written anything in. Tell me what you have in mind."

"I thought the Red Cross or county nurses could talk to us about how to stay healthy, how to prevent mothers and babies from dying in childbirth. Things like that. I read that many people test positive for TB in our area and that it is a preventable disease. Maybe they can teach us how to prevent it."

Well, I guess I deserved the look he gave me, but I had my Health Club. I guess that really started to make my dream of being a nurse come true. On my way out, I asked if I he would announce that there was going to be a health club so kids could sign up, and also was I tall enough to be a Crossing guard. He said, "Yes, we provide a tall Stop sign and a bright vest for safety."

"May I still check that on the form?"

4

EVERY BIRD MUST
LEAVE THE NEST

Family Sacrifices

I was so happy when all my family attended my ninth grade graduation and award ceremony. For some reason our class was seated in the balcony in the back of the auditorium. At the awards ceremony, we had to climb down, walk the length of the room, climb up the stairs of the stage and then go back. Maybe they wanted us and our family to bask longer in our moment of glory.

After my second award, the Superintendent, Mrs. Florence Scott, who had appeared to be asleep on the stage, put her arm in my path as I started to return to my seat. I was startled, thinking I had done something wrong. She put her arm around my waist and whispered,

"Don't go back to the balcony, stay close the stage." Do you know how awkward that was for me? I sensed my family's discomfort, and saw my classmates whispering to each other and some even signaling me to come back. It all became clear of course, when I had to climb to the stage for six more certificates and the Science Medal for outstanding project.

Years later, I learned that my parents had been told by the principal and some of my teachers, after the reception, that I needed a bigger school with more resources, that I had a lot of potential. I had already done 12th grade work and projects, read every book in the library, including reference books and the Bible which I could not check out. They were reassured that I would get scholarships for college.

One afternoon, within a few weeks after school ended, my parents told me to get in the big truck that was parked in front of our house. We were moving to Corpus Christi where my brothers had bought a home for us. "My things??" Already in the truck. I must have been reading when they packed their things and furniture and even chickens in the truck.

I never asked and my family never explained why the move was not discussed with me. Perhaps they were afraid that I would run off with the Senior boy who had invited me to his Prom. My cousin was invited by his best friend. They thought they would pick us up together, but the only way we were allowed to go was for my Tío Matilde to take us. He had double parked his car by the door to the hall and leaned on the wall by the entrance the whole time. He never took his eyes off of me and my cousin. I was sure the only reason I had been invited was because the guys knew that my cousin would not be allowed to go by herself.

I was only fourteen, but I was profoundly aware of the great sacrifice my parents and brothers made for me. Six generations of our family had lived in that little village, their only experience out of there was to work in the fields. It had not been a vacation on a resort. They lived in tent camps and charged out of their meager weekly earnings. Hardly adequate preparation for life in the big city. Thank God that my siblings had left after they finished school, first to Chicago and then to Corpus Christi. I think it dawned on them how much they had to help us adjust, when we got to Corpus late in the evening and they realized my mother had brought her chickens in the truck. My sister lived in a small town on the outskirts, so she inherited them around midnight.

Ventured Out With Training Wheels

Moving to Corpus Christi from Salineño, Texas, was a huge culture shock for my parents and me. That my siblings had established lives there and were invested in having us close helped tremendously. Three of them bought houses on the same street. The neighborhood was mostly Hispanic. I consider that move my baby steps in venturing out, with training wheels on. They wanted a better education for me, but more importantly they recognized that my parents needed better access to medical care. Our family was all together, providing a safe zone for me.

My biggest joy was reuniting with Nash and Eddie, my nephews. My father, though recuperating from a surgery that saved his life for a strangulated hernia and restricted medically from labor, dug up our entire backyard to plant vegetables and make flower beds for my mother's roses and hibiscus's. He almost moved back, but my brother found him a job at the Naval Air Station where he worked. Papa worked for another 15 years. My mother, being a more resigned person, was actually ecstatic in the fabric and crafts sections of Solo-Serve and Weiner's, and grocery shopping at HEB. She visited the chickens she had brought with her at my sister's house. Soon she was holding craft and quilting lessons for the neighbor ladies in the garage. She joined the Guadalupana Society at church. I got involved with Faith Formation and social activities through Catholic Youth Organization (CYO).

Once I started school I was happy. I found the differences more interesting than challenging, and I made friends fast and they were glad to help me navigate. One of those friends, Sylvia, lived three houses down the street across from my brother. She told me something a few years ago that made me cry: she said Mama had walked to their house to meet her mother and said, "Sra. Garcia, I need your help. We moved here to help my daughter get into a better school and find more challenging activities for her, but I don't know how. I can't help my daughter. Would you help me, please?" My friend added that my mother had choked up talking to her mother. That explained a huge part of why I had felt that I "vexed" my parents.

I was sitting looking dejected on the porch the next day and her mother told her to come over. She introduced herself and asked me, "What school are you going to go to, what grade are you in?" She says my eyes opened wide in surprise and I asked,

"There's more than one school?" That's when she took me under her wing.

When I started school there were over 460 students in the 10th grade with me. There had been 49 of us in the 9th grade in Roma. And the school was much more diverse. One big issue that bothered me, (which for me meant figuring out how to fix it) was that though there was no open hostility among the groups, they maintained themselves separate. I spoke to everyone, and even continued talking to a class-mate unaware that we had walked into her group. I became aware that prejudice and discrimination are two way highways, heading towards me on my own lane. I was called a "Coconut" by Hispanic friends for mingling with Anglos. There was another name given to me for talking to "Blacks". The word "Black" was usually spoken in a whisper.

It was the first year (1955) that Blacks were accepted into the two white High Schools as a result of an anti-segregation lawsuit. Though we had had the Anglo "Dam Children" in Roma, those children were used to being the "new kid on the block" because of the nature of their fathers' civil engineering professions. They made the first overtures to adapt and be friends, and we were open to welcoming them and eager to learn from them. That was not the dynamics in our High School.

I met more hostility when I joined the Future Nurses Club, the Jr. Red Cross Club and was selected to Student Council from my Homeroom. To make things worse, I was elected an Officer in each one. It didn't help matters when they found out that I was volunteering as a Candy Striper at the County hospital. At that time most High School age Hispanics held jobs to help their families, which meant that few had time to participate in sports or extracurricular activities and still maintain their grades. They thought I must come from a rich family if I worked for free. Another reason I stood out was that my sisters sent me clothes from Chicago, although my mother still made some of my clothes from their cast downs, but followed the styles of the store bought ones my sisters sent.

I became the "Philosopher" because I was always trying to explain to my friends, that if we held ourselves apart, we were buying into the idea that we're not "equals". We are all created in the image of God, so we must not feel that we are less than others. Also, I said we had to participate more in extracurricular activities, like the production of the annual and newspaper, in the school play and other things.

What my friends also didn't understand, was that I envied them the experience of working in a store or hamburger place. I was not allowed to go out without one of my brothers chaperoning me so I used the excuse that I had another commitment when I was invited. I had to quit the marching band, which I had joined in Roma, playing trombone ordered through the Sears catalog. After the first year, when my parents learned that the band went to play out of town with the athletic teams, they wanted me to quit right away, but I promised I would not sign up for band the next year.

My family and I did develop a plan to finance my college and Nursing School education. Two of my brothers had taken advantage of the GI Bill to learn trades that would lead to employment at the Corpus Christi Army Depot and the third brother took Auto Mechanics at the Technical School. Since no one in the family had attended a University, we did not know how to prepare for that or that planning should have started already.

My sister- in -law had studied at the local Beauty College and had her own shop. So at the end of my 10th Grade I enrolled there, to attend summers full time and Saturdays during the school year, with a promise from my sister-in-law that she would let me work part-time when I got my license. My nephew and I started working part time with her, sweeping up and cleaning the instruments, so I could go to the Jr. College first, then to a Nursing School. My father never owned a car, so my brothers committed to drive me to and from the Beauty College, and I moved my candy striper work to Sundays.

If you had a Hispanic name, you were Mexican and "Mexicans" were not expected to be too smart. In fact, when my school administered an IQ test to all the students taking Latin I, II and III, a "Mexican" boy and I had to take it again, watched by four proctors. No one explained why, except for my Solid Geometry and Algebra teacher, Mr. Bohannon. He said we had scored above everyone, surprisingly and unacceptably to the powers that be, and that I scored 17 points higher the second time around. I laughed and said "Give it to me again and I will score 34 points higher." Then I got angry, realizing that the proctors were there to make sure we had not cheated. He said not to let anything or anyone hold me back. He said I had a wide range of right brain and left brain aptitudes and could be a maid or a brain surgeon; that it was up to me. (Surprisingly, my son was also tested and found that his left and right brain were equally developing as toddler.) He studied Computer Engineering but has taught himself plumbing, electricity and construction to keep up with his rental properties. He even took Art Appreciation as an elective.

Toward the end of my senior year, I was beginning to overhear some of my classmates say that they had been accepted to University X and offered a scholarship. When I asked Mr. Bohannon, my Algebra teacher, how they were able to do that, he told me to go talk to my counselor, and gave me her name. When I went, she was very dismissive: "Your parents can't afford college for you." When I explained that I was attending Beauty College already, so I could work my way through Nursing School, she said,

"Beautician is good occupation for Mexican girls. You're just going to have lots of kids and your husband won't let you work. You can make money cutting hair at home." She had my file in front of her, at this point she could have told me about class rankings, and that I would graduate in the top 2.5% of the class and qualify for scholarships. But she didn't. My name was included in the Graduation Program which simply broke out the names of the top 10% in alphabetical order. The Valedictorian and Salutatorian were a Mexican girl and an Anglo girl. Had I only known about class rankings, and that extra credit work was available for top ranked students to break ties or just to see who were the most committed!!

Furious, I left her office, took the bus to the three year nursing school run by the Sisters of Charity of the Incarnate Word and took the entrance exams three days later. The nun, Sister Christiana, who did the pre-admission interview three weeks later, asked me, "How are your parents planning on financing your tuition and fees?" I told her my plan and she "sadly" told me that their students were not allowed to work. The course load was too heavy. Once we went through the basic nursing skills classes we could work one shift a week as an aide for minimum pay, if our grades were good. Then she asked me if I was interested in knowing how I'd done in the exams. I responded that I was just thanking God that I had passed and that I would get back to her on the finances. She laughed, I stood up to leave, and I guess she could see I was angry, misinterpreting her laughter. She said sternly, "Sit."

That's when she told me that my scores in the five section test, had ranged in the 96 to 98 percentile, and explained what that means. She said that I would get a full academic scholarship because of my scores and my GPA on the HS transcript, which meant that I had to maintained grades above B at all times. She reassured me that she did not doubt I would be able to handle that. Also she said that the scholarship covered room and board, I was required to live in the dorms, though I lived in town and that uniforms were not covered by the school, but that they were laundered by the hospital for free. I would also need money for personal expenses. After I regained my voice, I asked if it was permissible to cut my classmates' hair or do their nails for spending money, and she again laughed, "I think they would do me bodily harm if I stopped you."

My brother Luis would also give me $3.58 every 15 days, which I assume was the odd sum of his paycheck.

Reflections:

1. Who were the angels in my life who affirmed me and helped me attain my full potential?

2. Do I see God's hand in my life and do I give Him thanks for putting those angels in my path?

3. Have I been God's angel for others? Do I hear him calling me to help others?

Freedom is a Dangerous Thing

My parents could not understand why I had to stay at the Nursing School Dorms since we lived in town. When I explained that it was because the course work at the Junior College and at the school was a lot, plus I had to study and rotate helping the priest distribute the Eucharist to the patients at 7 AM. My brothers backed me up on this, since they were the ones who would have to drive me around. They asked me to call them every day, but I needed to come home on weekends.

Life in the dorms was like a slumber party every night, though I had never really experienced that. I also had a nice clientele that kept me busy with cutting hair and styling, manicures and facials, especially since the girls soon were dating locally or their hometown boyfriends came to see them. I think I was the only one who rejoiced at the 10 PM curfew on school nights and midnight on weekends. All we had to do was sign the book if we were going out, what time left, time returning and a brief explanation for going out. I noticed that everyone just wrote date, parents in town, and ice cream parlor. My parents had not even let me go out at all, so I did not need a curfew. The school owned six bikes and we could sign them out on weekends if we went to study at Del Mar College or just across the street at the shoreline park and bike trails.

I was in heaven, until ...

At mid-term Sr. Christiana called me to her office. No, I wasn't failing but, my grades were not what she had expected of me, based on my entrance exam scores. She really reamed me out and said, "You should be making straight A's, you're a genius, brilliant even (which is it I thought). And by the way you did not graduate in the top 10% of your class, you were in the top 2.5%. She studied my folder and noticed that I had answered the question on the application: are you handicapped or need special assistance in taking these exams? I had written in: I broke my glasses two days ago and won't be able to get new ones until the end of the month.

She looked at my glasses and exclaimed, "My God child, you are wearing coke bottle bottoms for glasses." I have extreme astigmatism. She said, "You don't have to, but I'm curious how you would do if you took the test with your glasses on." Stupid me, I was curious too, so I took the exams again. A week later she called me in and boy, did she really ream me out again. I had improved my scores by almost 40 points. I did not ask her what that meant, because she was threatening me that if I did not make A's or above this term she would not allow me to go home on weekends or to work. (That was tempting. My friends had come to pick me up at home last weekend, to go to Austin to meet my roommate's brother and his friend. The guy who was taking us, honked his horn for me to come out. Well my father came out with me and told the surprised young man, "A gentleman does not toot his horn. He comes to the door and knocks, meets a señorita's parents and assures them that he'll bring her back safe."

Nonetheless, I buckled down, went out less and studied more. I would never want to explain to my parents and brothers why I could not come home on weekends. I had considered it a miracle from God that I had passed the entrance exams and now I was even more amazed. Thank you, Jesus.

I graduated as the "Outstanding Graduate" three years later, which earned me another full scholarship to the Nursing program at Incarnate Word University (IWU) in San Antonio. The people of Salineño kept track of my life and used me as an example to their children, that they too could get an education and succeed. My cousin, Juan Escobar, who later became a Texas State Representative, his mother and brothers were at my graduation. He tells me that they were picking cotton in Chapman Ranch (Chapeño) near Corpus and his mother Rosita Vera, my mother's cousin, had them quit at noon, shower and come to the graduation. She told them, "We are going to Corpus to Belzita's graduation from Nursing School. She was born in Salineño, so you can see that you don't have to pick cotton all your life."

Upon graduation, I could not take my State Boards with my classmates, because I was not yet 21. I waited out a semester, in order to focus on my boards, plus, I also wanted to see the Pediatric Ward that an RN and I had created, for my senior project, as a functioning unit. In that interim I met someone stationed at the Navy base and he asked me to marry him before I went to IWU. We agreed that he would pursue becoming a Catholic, before formalizing an engagement. After three months, he had not even initiated the process, so I broke up with him.

At IWU, I was taking a heavy load, working full-time and volunteering with the local Red Cross Chapter. I say that I graduated without "honors". Infrequently I went out with my roommate's brother and two of his roommates (separately). Though they raced each other to get to the phone to call me before the weekend, they were like brothers to me. I was surprised when we all graduated and I had accepted a job with the American Red Cross (ARC), two of them proposed. Not the right time.

For Reflection:

1. Who has shown "tough love" with me and not let me just get by, knowing I am capable of more?

2. Am I able to discipline myself and buckle up to achieve my goals?

3. Can family expectations and gratitude to God be motivating factors?

Crossroads–A Three-way Moment

Did we know this moment was at a crossroad in our lives?
A three-way moment that must be captured.
For it may never come again.
Walking on the wet sand, our body mirrored ahead of us, our shadow cast at an angle,
Made two perfect right-angles.
On this happy day at the beach.

The three of us were enjoying our youth
Though their aunt, growing up together, just
Four and seven years older than they.
Celebrating with them the freedom only a college diploma,
A new job and a new car can bring.
At the beach, playing yet conscious to set a good example,
Anticipating life with its joys and successes.
Loss and suffering not in our horizon.

Only in retrospect does the question arise:
How could we know what lay ahead?
Protective aunt barely an adult moving away.
Would we mindfully choose our way?
Our only certainty: *la familia es sagrada.*
We'd always support and spur each other on.
Together or apart, pulling ourselves up by our bootstraps.

At the Beach

5

WHAT WAS I THINKING

A Lifelong Dream I Did Not Fight For

My childhood girl friends and I loved to play out our detailed fantasies of our dream wedding. We commandeered one of their brothers or one of my nephews to stand in as a groom and priest, for it must be Catholic wedding and it was a given that we would marry a Catholic man.

Both friends married after I moved to Corpus Christi. One invited me to her Methodist wedding and the other one didn't invite me. I was surprised and hurt when I found out that she married a man twice her age, but well off. Their marriages were "forever". Their children are successful adults now and they also have good marriages.

I eventually had more ideas of the kind of man I wanted to marry. He would be Hispanic or at least speak Spanish, a Catholic, and a professional but not in the medical field. He would come from a large family and we'd have like political views or at least we'd be tolerant of each other's. Our wedding would be at the Cathedral in Corpus, performed by the Bishop. I wanted to have my Master's degree and a specialization in Pediatric Nursing and be established in my career, probably be over thirty years old.

Needless to say, I learned some hard lessons along the way and even doubted I would marry. It was not a problem that my parents did not allow me to date in high school, because Hispanic boys were not interested in me in high school. Anglo boys who even spoke to me only wanted me to help them with their homework or projects.

My nursing schoolmates and I went out in groups with boys at Del Mar college, some of whom I'd known in High School. The Nuns allowed us to host summer dances for the Midshipman classes from the Naval Air Station. Some long term courtships and eventual marriages emerged from that, but not for me.

In my senior year I went out with a Turkish Resident with a nurse and her husband, a Filipino doctor. On the second date he said that women are not emotionally constituted to make it in life alone, that's why they need a man. I just got up and left.

Life on the Margin

I did not cross a river or an ocean.
But boundaries I did jump.
Caught at cross currents of brown and white waters,
Tossed about like an uprooted stump.
Trying to grab a stronghold
In the land where I was born.
Yet hold on to beautiful *tradiciones* from another world,
Nurtured with love, planted in my soul.

Ventured out to that vast outside world.
A few hands stretched out to bless or welcome.
Why do you want in? Why do you want out?
Why don't you stay in your mold?
How can I be that bridge across those waters?
When I'm the one who needs it,
To cross over before I sink.
And back again lest I become an island.

Ventured Out into Uncharted Territory

My volunteer work with the San Antonio Chapter of the American Red Cross (ARC) teaching Mother and Baby Care to expectant parents led to being hired by the ARC at the National level as the first Hispanic National Nursing Representative. They first sent me for nine weeks' training in St. Louis, their headquarters. Other than going with my family as a child to pick cotton in Missouri and Mississippi, I had never been out of Texas. I took a couple of weeks off after graduation from IWU, to spend with my family in Corpus, get some clothes and a suitcase and say goodbye to my nephews. I was a bit apprehensive of driving by myself, but tried to not let on. A couple of days before I left, with an Atlas and AAA map routes laid out, my oldest brother and his wife, Rene and Mary, said they would drive me to St. Louis in my car and return by bus to Corpus. They insisted it was an adventure for them.

The ARC had arranged for me to stay at a nearby hotel. The first day of training, I found myself as the only woman with nine men. They were also National Reps but in different areas like Disaster Assistance, Water Safety, etc. They were nice young men, but not as young and naïve like me. Most were married, showing pictures of wives and kids. We got into the habit of meeting half an hour after classes ended to walk or take two taxis to a nearby restaurant for supper. On weekends we explored St. Louis in smaller groups, depending on how many did not go home to their families and on our interests. They were very gentlemanly and surrounded me when we walked. As we got to know each other, they were very curious about me, realizing I'd had a very sheltered life. I shared that my parents were of Spanish descent, and that my ancestors were some of the original land grantees from the King of Spain. They started calling me princess. I felt comfortable and accepted with them, and yes even protected.

Around the second week, one young man started to try to separate us from the group, which I resisted. For the weekend, only four of us wanted to go see the now famous St. Louis arches, being put up. He was one of them. As we walked, he said I was too naïve and that I should try to get some experience. I said I was, learning a different field of nursing and getting to know different people in this state. The others approached and we walked around some more before returning to the hotel. In the middle of the week he called me before I went down to the lobby to meet for supper. He said that we were going to a really nice restaurant, that required reservations and some were going ahead to try to get a table. But he was the only one waiting. I did not think anything of it and we took a taxi. When we got to the "restaurant" two men were checking ID's, which I did think odd. (Of course, I'd been to nice restaurants before!!) The checker looked at my license for a long time, then said, "Texas, huh? What are you doing in St. Louis? I told him, and my co-worker said impatiently, that I was with him.

In the dimly lit room with small round tables, I wondered how we all are going to sit together, looking for the others. He said, they must have decided to go somewhere else and we sat down. All of a sudden the room got darker, music started. That's when I realized there was a stage and a woman was up there beginning to take her clothes off. (Of course, my mother's voice said, "Get out of here. You're in a Strip Club.") Of course I'd heard of strip joints. I excused myself, needing to go to the ladies room.

I walked up to the checker and told him I needed a taxi. He walked out with me, hailed a taxi, and said, "I knew you were not the type for this place, but you are of age." He opened the door for me and went around to the front to talk to the driver, a fatherly type. I was too upset, almost in tears. He asked where I was staying, talked some more to the driver. When we got to the hotel, I looked at the meter and took out a bill to cover it. He said I did not have to pay, that the checker had already paid. I was really crying then, but told him to please thank him for me and that I said "God Bless him." He said, "Don't be so trusting."

The next evening, I told the guys I was not joining them for supper, I was behind with my studying. The second evening, one of the guys took me aside after class and said, "Look we've already talked to that jerk and he told us what he did, how you'd left and he did not even know how you'd gotten back to the hotel. He will not be joining us any more, ever, and please don't think we're all like him. We will never let anything like that happen to you. We want you to come with us to dinner, ok?" I said I would, but not tonight. I was going to thank God for all the angels he was surrounding me with.

The next day a woman joined us in class, introduced herself as the Director of the St. Louis ARC Chapter. Florence said she needed a refresher and would be with us for the rest of the course. I rented a room from her and we rode in together from then on. I could not expect my co-workers to baby-sit with me.

Looking back to that very unpleasant experience, I realize that God has an army of angels to look after his beloved children even if they are already 23. Sometimes the angels have your mother's voice so you can obey them. I can think of many other occasions when I just had a feeling something was not for me and stayed away. I also thank Him that I did learn my lesson and nothing really bad happened to me. It reminds me of my father always sharing an "on the other hand" story when he shared stories of discrimination and just bad people. On the other hand, there are good people in this world.

Really Way Out There Without Any Armor

When our training ended, the ARC sent me to the Minneapolis-St. Paul Chapter on a project until an opening became available as a District Nursing Representative. The project was to get all the Red Cross courses on Public Access TV and to procure places like schools, community centers etc. where people could come and practice the skills taught in the courses with a live instructor. This meant I was out and about a lot in the cold and driving in the snow. I had rented the lower half of a farm home owned by the Director closer to St. Paul than to Minneapolis where the Red Cross offices were, so I had a good drive just to get to the office.

She and other women really were very nice and helped me adapt to the area and to the cold. I had never driven in snow or even experienced such cold. When I told them about my car skidding on ice when I came in one morning, they told me about snow tires and one went with me at lunch to get them installed. They also showed me their thermal wear and where to buy it, when I came in peeling off layers of sweaters. I could handle the fact that my nose, ears, knees and finger tips nearly froze and were peeling all the time, but breathing in the cold air, was causing me to cough a lot. A doctor told me I had thermal allergy, which caused my lungs to go into spasms, but that I would get over it eventually.

One of the younger women invited me to join a women's bowling league and went with me to get a ball and shoes. We ended up winning and she gave a party to celebrate. The women asked her to invite some single men and she did. That is how I met my husband. Falling in love did not wait until I was thirty and did not care to befall on my "dream man." When I realized he did not meet what I wanted in the person I married, especially that he was a non-believer, and had been married before, I stopped seeing him. He was very persistent and I really had never experienced anyone being that interested in me.

By this time, I had been with the ARC almost a year, and was informed that there was an opening in North Dakota and that's where I would be assigned. I turned in my resignation, because I realized I missed the hospital environment, had not adapted to the cold and my research told me North Dakota would be even colder. I also wanted to put distance between this man I had met and fallen in love with. I knew he was not for me.

I had no problem getting a job at the Public Hospital in Corpus, and my family was happy to have me back. He called me every day when I returned to Texas and pursued me in an elaborate and probably expensive long distance courtship. If my parents picked up, they handed the phone to me saying "your boyfriend" and I would say "he's not my boyfriend." Telling them the truth about him was not something I could talk to my parents about. I felt diminished that I had made such a big mistake in character judgment.

I prayed to God to guide me out of love and that I would meet my "dream man". I did start dating someone else, but my parents were appalled. They voiced concerns that I had had "too many boyfriends" and should either marry my boyfriend who called every day or become a nun.

"Our family does not do those things. You will be viewed as a "used woman", they said.

Deaf and Blind Decision

After two years, not dating anyone else, I married my non-dream man in a civil ceremony at home in November 1965. I did love him and he seemed amenable to converting to Catholicism "sometime", and letting me pursue my career and studies. God gave me many signals that he was not the right man for me, but I did not listen. Love tends to blind you and affect your hearing. Love also makes you believe you have super powers to change someone. I simply did not have the skills or confidence to handle the situation. My faith was not informed enough to consider talking to a priest.

We drove back up to Minneapolis after we got married, pulling a U-Haul with my Encyclopedia Britannica, uniforms and shoes, and little else. We moved into a townhouse whose parking lot adjoined the parking lot of a hospital. It was already snowing and freezing and I'd rather walk across two parking lots, than drive. They offered me a supervisory job but being newly married I did not want the responsibility, although I had to do all three shifts as a staff nurse. I was happy to be assigned to patient care in the pediatric unit. Even before I got out of school, I had been given charge assignments when I worked a shift, and to set up a pediatric unit as a senior project with and RN. I was evening charge in the six months before starting at IWU.

After a month they asked me to develop a skills training course for new graduates of two year nursing schools and to supervise them for at least three months. Two years of schooling did not provide sufficient skills training, but because of the severe shortage of nurses, it was a good alternative, as long as hospitals assumed responsibility for providing further skills training. I felt responsible for helping provide that, but it was still shift work.

The rude awakening with my marriage was quick and heartbreaking. Within six weeks I learned that almost everything my husband had ever told me about himself was false. He had not been single when we met, had only obtained a divorce a couple of months before we married. He had told me he had two kids from a "previous" marriage, but actually had three. He rescinded every promise he'd ever made. He never came home right after work.

One evening my brother-in-law called me that he was on his way to North Dakota to put up an oil rig but had a four hour layover in Minneapolis. I was not working but did not know my way around too well. He said no problem, he would take a taxi. He could tell right away that I was miserable, especially when it was close to ten and my husband was not home, had not called. I am not good at lying and just opened up to my brother-in-law. He said, "Look, you've made a mistake. If you want to come back to Texas when I come by here in two weeks, you can fly home with me or we can drive your car back. Carmen and I will support you if you can't face *los viejitos* (my parents)."

However, I found that my culture was so much a part of me, that I decided to stay. I could not face my family with my failure after all the sacrifices they had made for me. Marriage was supposed to be forever, even a civil one, and subconsciously I felt that there was not a "dream man" out there for me. I really had had very little experience with dating, so I had no basis for feeling that way.

We moved to Puerto Rico (PR) with his job when we'd been married eight months and I was four months pregnant. Within three years of marriage, I had my daughter and son, a great Nanny, and my nursing career was going great, with a promise of becoming Director of Nursing. At the request of President Johnson's Administration, my boss allowed me to split my shift to be a consultant to the Labor Department to develop and implement a one year training program for medical and nursing auxiliary personnel at the PR Medical Center. It was even beneficial for me to be accessible in the Nursing Office for two hours into the evening shift.

My boss got really excited about that call and after a call from the WHO to inquire if I was interested in heading a start-up in Columbia for a nursing school. She asked if I was on some kind of list. I had no idea. She wanted me to get my PR Nursing license, because the hospital was going to be converted into a two level nursing home for seniors and we were working with an architectural firm for that and to build a new hospital facility. She said that if I got my license, I would be the Director of Nursing.

My children were going to start Kindergarten, full time soon, so I took a leave of absence to spend some time with them before undertaking more responsibility. I needed time as well to wage a fight with PR (the state department) for refusing to grant me a nursing license by reciprocity. At that time Texas did not have a reciprocal agreement with PR. They finally informed me of this after losing my documents twice, and only after I requested a hearing. At the hearing they informed me that they only grant reciprocity from the original state license. I had gotten a license from Minnesota by reciprocity, but they would not consider that at that time. My only option was to take the Board exams in Spanish, so I had to hone up on my medical/technical Spanish.

I was contemplating divorcing my husband and needed to decide if I would stay in PR or return home to Texas, to Corpus or Houston. On one hand, a part of me was glued to ingrained cultural beliefs about marriage and had to consider that I would stay. I wanted to have all my options open. I just thanked God that He was giving me enough self-confidence for some tough decisions ahead.

Light Lifts the Darkness–My Crowning Moment

Options: Not many for my generation of Catholic women. You get married first, then have children if and when God wills it. You may ask God for a large or a small family, but you will accept "*Lo que Dios quiere.*" I believe that God has a plan for each of us and we need to be obedient and participate in it. I believe that you act on your beliefs.

A doctor had told me that I might not ever conceive and if I did conceive, he said, I would need a C-Section. My pelvic structure was that of an 8 or nine year old, probably due a severe illness. (Yes, I had all the childhood diseases at once, developed pleurisy, and was bed-ridden for three months.) I was not too discouraged, because in the end it would be "*Lo que Dios quiere.*" Besides, I was single then and not ready to get married.

But soon after, I met my husband and we got married. We talked about having a large family like mine. He said that as an only child he'd always wanted brothers and sisters, that we could afford a large family and to have a nanny to help. We did agree to wait a year to start our family. I had shared with him what the doctor had told me, but for good measure, I tried to practice natural family planning, the only option for me. Within four months of marriage, I was expecting. Ecstatic, after my OB-Gyn confirmed it, I planned a nice dinner, with all his favor-ites, steak, baked potato, all the trimmings. I added candles, soft music.

That he was not very happy about the news is a gross understatement. I had agreed to wait a year. **Option:** I was going to have this baby, but he was free to do whatever he wanted. My mother love came out fighting, but it was not an easy pregnancy. Maybe because of my state of mind or because I was doing shift work at the hospital, I had twenty-four hour "morning sickness" for three months. I lost weight instead of gaining. When I was four months pregnant, we moved to PR with my husband's job. On the flight, I used all the air sickness bags on the plane. A doctor on the flight gave me a pill for nausea and told the flight attendants to keep giving me water or juice. I felt better by the time we landed, but a few days later something I ate made me sick again, requiring IV fluids in the emergency room.

A month later when our furniture arrived, I started setting it up by myself and I started having contractions. Our cars had not arrived, so my husband was riding with another manager at his company, who lived down the block from us. Soon after they left, Carlos' wife, Mare, showed up and took me to the OB doctor, recommended to me in Minnesota. After we left the doctor's, we got the medicine he prescribed. Mare fed me, then took me home and put me in bed as the doctor ordered. She brought dinner later. God was building a support group for me.

Options: Marriage is forever, you made your bed you lay in it; divorce – we don't do that in our family. Things were not going well with my marriage. I decided that going to work would help my mental state. I applied at two hospitals and got job offers, even though I let them know I'd have to go on Maternity Leave in four months. I took the job offered by the Catholic Hospital, training staff to operate a new Intensive Care Unit. This could only be a God-incidence, that the hospital had an urgent need and I showed up at the right time, with experience in starting up a pediatric unit, an ICU **and** training nursing personnel for a new hospital wing **and** bi-lingual. *Dios protégé los suyos.*

I talked to my OB-GYN about having a natural delivery. I wanted to be conscious for the baby's birth. He said it was possible if the baby stayed small. He would arrange for a C-Section, just in case. My baby was due January 7th, but on December 23rd my husband and I had an argument about him attending the company Christmas Party. It was going to be up in the mountains, and he wanted to go by himself. His logic: "What if you go into labor, we have to come down the mountain, and 20 miles back in to San Juan?"

"Then you should not even go. If I do go into labor, how will I get to the hospital?" He was determined to go, so I reminded him that the due date was two weeks away anyway. I just prayed I would not go into labor. He went out and the car would not start. He called for a rental, and it was never delivered. I was thankful to God but devastated about his lack of concern for me and the baby and suspect of why he wanted to go by himself.

Around 3 AM we both woke up on a very wet mattress. My water broke! He tried to start the car again without any luck. He ran down the block without his shoes to borrow Carlos's car, hoping they'd be back from the party. At the hospital, labor pains did not start until about 7:30 AM. My doctor suggested inducing me. Since the water broke early he feared infection as I well knew. I said let's wait twenty minutes, and thank God, I went into hard labor almost immediately.

Within an hour and a half, he yelled "Baby is crowning." So far I was confident that I could go through it without drugs. All of a sudden I was fighting with my doctor and the stand-by anesthesiologist. They were trying to put me under!! I yelled "Wait, I can stand the pain. I want to be awake when my baby is born." But that's all I remember until 5 PM, December 24th, when the nurse came in and said "Wake up, wake up, let's see if you can feed this hungry baby girl." The nurse had a bottle of formula.

She said that she was born at 11:52 AM, and that they had to put me under because the baby's crown looked very blue. They knew that the cord was around her neck, common in dry labors and had to use instruments to turn her. She reassured me my beautiful Renée Therese was fine. After a few tries, Renée succeeded in her mission. As her hunger was satisfied, we both relaxed. I looked around the room and to my surprise the origami Christmas decorations I had made and grabbed before we came to the hospital, were hung on the curtains and walls.

The nurse saw my smile and said some nuns from Auxilio Mutuo, where I was working, had come in and put them up. As we were settling Renée back on her bassinette, a nun came in, with a small bag with her knitting and prayer books. *Feliz Navidad, Sra. Ramos-Long.* She introduced herself and said she was spending every night with us. We stayed in the hospital for three days and two or three nuns and supervisors came to visit during the day. God was sending more angels to build my support group.

My beautiful Renée Therese was the best Christmas present I ever got. She was my crowning moment. It made me humble, thanking God for this new life, for the Doctor's quick thinking to rescue her during birth, and for both of us coming through it all. For her and my son, and with them, I grew up, faced the future less naïvely, giving more thought to tough decisions I had to make, and started on my motherhood journey. I began to pray to God for guidance in being a good mother.

HAIKUS –CHOOSE LIFE

Birth Control

Responsible plan?
Or sacrifice my values?
Or justified need?

Woman's Role

A mate for Adam.
Lead or follow, teach or learn
Love, hope for mankind.

No Abortion

Your seed from my tree-
Nurtured in our orchard,
Not killed by the tiller's blade.

Abortion

Child interrupted.
Hole in the soul forever
Never to be whole.

Adoption

Give away a gift
Priceless, non-returnable.
Eager hopefuls wait.

Pregnancy

Mystery of life
Center of gravity shifts.
Self-centered no more.

Expectant woman:
Partner in God's creation
Expect perfection.

Infertility

Years on birth control
Unaware unnecessary?
Or tragic result?

Hope for one baby to hold.
Oops, need four more laps.

Mothers

Partners in God's plan
Center of gravity shifts.
Care more for another.

Win/Win Solution:
Adoption stops abortion!
Mission: Godlier humans.

A Second Bundle of Joy

My son, Antonio Luis, was born twenty-two months after my daughter at Auxilio Mutuo Hospital, with the same OB-GYN and Pediatrician in attendance. This time I did not say anything about natural childbirth. I told both of them that my husband definitely did not want any more babies, told the pediatrician I wanted to breast feed at least for six months. I had an easier pregnancy and uneventful birth this time and went home within 24 hours. The nurse, following the pediatrician's orders let me nurse Tony twice before we went home even though the OB-GYN had given me a shot to dry up my milk in the delivery room.

I was giving Tony water in between the breast feedings, but I noticed that the "milk" was almost clear. He seemed satisfied for a few days, but both the nanny and I noticed that with the slightest noise his little arms and legs would shake. She said this baby is very nervous, and we both kept a close eye on him. One afternoon I breast fed him, and he fell asleep, so I laid him down in the crib and came out and started reading the paper. Something made me put down the paper immediately and go to the nursery. His arms and legs were contracting but he was conscious, his eyes not rolling back or anything. I called the hospital and told them I was bringing him in to ER and for them to call the pediatrician, describing why. Since I worked there my boss Sr. Clotilde called wanting to know if I wanted her to send someone to drive us. As usual my husband was not home from work, though it was almost 7 P.M. I left him a note. I thanked her and told her the nanny was already in the car with him and with Renee and I was locking up. It would save time.

In the ER, the pediatrician, the OB-GYN and a Pediatric Neurologist, were waiting for us, as well as my boss. Other doctors I had gotten to know in the ICU training were hanging around. The encephalogram did not show any abnormality, but the blood work indicated his electrolytes were low when they should high, high when they should be low. We all sat together so I could tell them again what had happened when. When I said I was breast feeding, the pediatrician did not react but the OB-GYN did with the fact that I had gotten a shot to dry up my milk. We all realized at the same moment that Tony was malnourished and going into tetany. He was immediately given IVs with electrolytes, a bottle with formula and an anti-convulsive. The Pedi-Neuro wanted to follow him up for six months to a year, just to make sure and prescribed a mild anti-convulsive. I got a copy for Dr. Firpi's feeding protocols and we went home when the IV was finished.

Tony was followed up for a year and half, with all exams and developmental milestones being normal, except walking. At a year the Neurologist scared me when he said Tony's left brain was over developing, but quickly explained that normally we tend to be right brained or left brained, some us tend to be both with high IQ, and both right brained aptitudes and interests equally developing. I mentioned how I had taught myself to use my right hand and left hand equally. He said I could test you but I already know what I would find. After three encephalograms six months apart and everything testing normal, Tony was off all medicine.

Tony did not walk until he was two, while his sister had raised up her little rump up off the floor than her arms and ran about three feet, when she was 9 months old. When my parents came to visit they noticed that the new nanny kept him in the playpen almost all day. My parents started to take him out, one on each side of him holding his hands to walk him. They only stayed for two months and he was walking fine.

He always dismantled every toy he got and soon was able to put them back together. When we started the electronic manufacturing company, he could pass a Sudoku-type test I designed with tiles in 4 different shapes and 4 different colors, to observe how prospective employees would organize the shapes and colors so they would not be repeated in any row. They did not have to actually "solve it". Tony at four could solve it in less than a minute and a half.

I would pay Tony and Renée a nickel for every simple assembly they put together after they did their homework and before we took the 45 minute drive home from the factory. Renée was not interested. Tony was and had money in his piggy bank.

When we left PR Tony was almost 9 years old and Renée almost 11. Tony went to all the neighbors asking for work so he could help "Mom, because now we only have her income." He offered to fix fans, lawn mowers, radios and lamps, as well as paint fences and mow and he did.

Though I had wanted a large family, I was thankful that the two I had were a boy and a girl and that even though I'd had some scary moments with them at birth or shortly after, they were healthy normal kids. When I left their father, I felt so dejected, but I would try to be strong for them. It worked, it was for them that I had left and for them that I would make it work. I held on to God's promise that He would not leave me orphan.

inner storm in paradise

sailed in waters serene and calm
curious fish big small beautiful menacing
eyeing us eyeing them
gentle trade winds filled our sails
cooling my skin
sun and friends my soul balm

toward private paradise
nestled in coral rainbow reef
swam with black silver gold and pearly fish
front seat view of anemones and sea urchin
ballerinas
yeah a seahorse takes a bow
inner turmoil deceptively calmed

picnic under regal palms
on tiny white sandy haven
good company good food good music
piña colada and scotch with coconut milk
no detail left out
daring to dream this my reality forever

followed golden path of setting sun
or silver road of rising moon
heading home as gusts of inner storm rear up
words thinly mask jealous rage
that someone dared snorkel with me
or found my food worthy of praise
evaporating my short-lived wholeness

I exited island paradise with my children.
Regained inner peace and hope
To sail toward heaven till the end of the journey.

I Prolong the Inner Storm – At Crossroads

As fate would have it, my husband was fired, and grandiosely (or was it cowardly?), I thought I could not leave him while he was down. I jokingly suggested starting our own company and he took me up on that, but said he did not know the first thing about how to do that. Since I was on leave of absence from the hospital, I had time on my hands. I bought a three tome encyclopedia I found at Barnes and Noble on "articles of incorporation, stock plans and meetings". Step by step, I wrote a stock plan and filed articles of incorporation, with 23 committed stockholders, prepared a business prospectus to take to the bank and the PR economic development equivalent. I contacted IRS to get an Employer ID number and the Labor Department and went to a bank and got a line of credit (with a lien on our house that we could change once the company got under way).

I did not go with my husband and four engineer stockholders to the Departamento de Fomento Industrial because I did not fully understand the technical concepts of the targeted government contracts. They gave us the use of a factory building, and tax incentives. I was the majority stockholder, so as a Woman-owned Minority Company we targeted government set-asides in the electronics sector for minority businesses. I was the Corporate Secretary and Administrative Manager. Within three months we were manufacturing.

Before my leave was up, I called a Stockholders meeting to see if anyone would step up to manage the company so I could take the Nursing Licensing Exams in Spanish and return to the hospital and a Director of Nursing position waiting for me. The result was that no one stepped up and they did not want me to leave, some threatening to withdraw their commitment if I did. So I resigned from the hospital and prolonged my inner storm.

I totally grasped basic electronic concepts, hired and trained all employees, developed policies and procedures for all aspects of the business: administrative and technical, and cleaned the bathrooms if needed. This was during the Energy Crisis and many new and old companies were closing. We became a model company for the PR Economic Development Agency, and they would bring local and Third World startup companies to let me share how we managed to stay in business.

Whether the excitement of learning and doing something totally new to me, impacting the local economy and in a small way the global economy as well, or again not wanting to admit failure, I stayed in the marriage working with my husband, for eight more years! At three years, we were doing well enough to buy out six stockholders who wanted their capital back. I worked 8 hour days at the factory. We had a 45 minute commute both ways. I picked up my kids from school, put them in the conference room, until it was time to go home. After feeding them, helping with homework and putting them to bed, I put in up to 3 hours more, dealing with stateside suppliers and contractors in the states with earlier hours.

Truth be told, I had prayed that maybe working and building up something together for our future would improve our marriage. But he was not a good husband or father and he played mental games with me. As a result I developed a complex, that although I was smart at some things, I believed that I was not lovable. This was confirmed when our anniversary came close, I suggested to my husband that we take a long weekend off alone. I knew he would say no, but I had to hear it, but what he did say was too hard to bear.

"I am not interested in spending four days alone with you." I asked, "How can I change that would change your mind?"

"I am tired of hearing what a good and smart wife I have. Everything you try, turns out as well as if a person who is an expert and educated in that area, did it. **I just need six months to be free.**" The next morning, he told me that since I "insisted on being equal, he was going to contribute only half his salary to the household" and again reiterated that "he just wanted six months to be free." I knew then in my gut he had embraced the custom in PR of having a mistress and the "little house". The house with the wife and kids was the "Big House". This was it for me. It could have been so many other times before this one for me, and I might not have had this long lasting shame of enduring such dehumanizing treatment for so long, even knowing that the "sad situation" was not going to get me to heaven.

I remembered my father's words, *"Vas a sufrir mucho porque piensas como un hombre".* Was that the real problem? That I think like a man? But God created me, and He expects us to use our God-given talents for the good of all. I could not fake to be something other than who I am. I had to talk to someone! I could not just pick up and leave with my children. I had responsibilities with too many people. Besides, I would need to be able to survive and provide for my children when I left.

Though I went to church with my children, raised them Catholic, I was not involved in any ministries and did not receive the Eucharist. In fact, no one spoke to me about ministries or anything at church. The priest disappeared right after Mass. I could not confide on any one in my circle of acquaintances because we were all involved with the company and/or worked together. If the stockholders meeting I'd held at the start of the company was any indication, it certainly meant I could not talk to any of them. I could not talk to my family because, I thought, they would just say, you made your bed, you lay on it.

After much prayer, I went to my old boss at the hospital. As a nun, that was the closest I could come to talking to a priest. She listened and in the end, she advised that I needed to leave for my own sanity. If I lost that then I could not be a good mother for my children. She explained that because I had been under pressure from my culture, and still was, even the Church would not hold me to my marriage. She also gave me a good pep talk. Even then, I recognized that God was with me and she was an angel He had put in my path. She gave me the name of a lawyer, her nephew.

That night I was getting ready for bed brushing my hair (100 strokes!) in front of the mirror, but not really looking at myself, mulling over everything Sister C. had said. All of a sudden, I really looked at myself hard in the mirror. From deep within me, I heard, not an external voice, but a voice nonetheless,

"My child, you are not acting like the person I planned you to be. You must leave, you and your children deserve a different story. I will not leave you orphaned."

Dissonant Symphony of *El Coquis*

Moved to *La Isla Del Encanto*
A bride in love.
Expecting our first child,
Strolling arm in arm,
Under the a canopy of flamboyant trees,
Gilded silver by full moon
On stage, a rhythmic symphony of coquis

"Coqui-i-i, coqui"
Marked our steps, soothed our ears.
Lush vegetation and sounds
Inspired golden dreams
Of prosperity and everlasting bliss.

Golden dreams faded,
Unnourished, slowly drowned
With lies, neglect, and broken promises.
Searched for him on that Christmas Eve celebration
For employees and friends.
To dance a birthday dance at midnight,
With our daughter, as is the custom.
And wish our employees and families
A Very Merry Christmas.
I find his body linked to hers.
Under the palms, hidden from the moon.

The dissonant song of coquis
Screaming "Betray-ay-ee", ay-ee, ay-ee
Painful to my ears, to
My heart and wounded soul.
Yet, like a zombie, I performed.
Asked the band to play *Feliz Cumpleaños.*
A friend to dance with my daughter,
Took the mic, said what he should have said.
Told them to continue with the party for another hour.
But I had a long ride home with my children.
And we left. Why did he follow us home?

El Coquis / Tree Frog

Possibility in Dislocation

Dislocation crept into my circle of possibilities.
I tried to slam the door in her face,
Leave her outside my circle, but she persisted.
Think of me differently she said.
Dislocate, Separate.

You've built a place
Where you can be safe
Where you are comfortable
With tall walls to shield and protect you.
Isolate, Stagnate.

Where you live alone, cautious and lost.
Self-pity and self-doubt.
Guard your fort.
Faithful sentinels at the gate.
Negate, Self-hate.

What could happen?
If you let yourself escape.
If you leave your comfort zone?
Explore your possibilities?
Liberate, Relocate, and Find the Advocate

Leaving Is a Leap of Faith

It was hard then and hard for me to write about this, because besides the tremendous professional growth I experienced, I had my son and daughter, enjoyed watching them grow, being a mother, seeing the employees prosper over the years. The employees would invite me to their new apartment when they got out of the projects, or to their new home or the renovation of their old. They were loyal and thankful to the company. There were few workers' comp accidents, mostly pinched fingers when not using the safety guard on the wire coding and cutting machine. They came back to work at a reasonable recovery time, knowing I could have contested their eligibility for compensation. Each got a large bottle of Pinch upon return. I started a supervisory training program for each of the major contract lines.

I had credibility with our contractors and if I said one of their specs was not workable, they worked with us. I had caught one of our contractors sending us re-work on printed circuit boards that we had not worked on. We did not want to create discord and lose the contract, so I asked them for advice on "how to resolve this problem with a contractor". They gave me copies of their rework policy, of their quality control program, advice on marking our work so it would be recognizable *and* paid us for the rework. I never had to accuse them, but I let them keep their song.

Those years matured me and let me discover that God had given me strengths and talents that I had not even suspected I had. After seven years of managing our Company, the economy picked up and our company added another line for color-coding wire and cable. We held on to our contracts with Digital Equipment Corp. (DEC), Matsushita (Panasonic Brand), Technicon and various smaller contracts or re-work orders. I recommended that we pay dividends to our stockholders and they agreed.

I deposited my dividend check in Corpus Christi. I decided to hire a Controller and train him to replace me as Administrative Manager. In case I decided to leave I started sending half my salary to the bank in Corpus. In case I decided to stay in PR even after a divorce, (cowardice again in facing my family) to keep tabs on the company, I applied at the School of Medicine for the Hospital Administration Program and was accepted, on a scholarship and a promise of a part-time professorship after I got my Masters. I got credit for my nursing education and management experience.

The first night of class, my husband did not come home as promised, to stay with the children, who were eight and ten years old. I called him and he said he was on his way, to just tell the children to stay in the house and not open for anyone. We had iron bars on all windows and doors, they'd be safe, he said. He'd be home in less than ten minutes. I left, after calling a neighbor to watch the house, and returned within 40 minutes because we only got our books and syllabus for each class and were dismissed.

I found my kids outside with the bar-b-que skewers in their hands and all the gates open. They had run off some thieves removing the stereo from one of our cars. Their dad had never come home. When he did, we had a great argument, and he said he was not under any obligation to help me get another degree. We were doing well enough, and he did not have his degree. That was news to me!! With that he got so angry, he fell on the floor.

My yearning to return to my faith, as immature and unschooled as it had been before marrying and the confidence that God was calling me back to Him, helped me leave at the end of the kids' school year. I left with my two children and three suitcases, and a promise that he would ship some of my things later, specially the Encyclopedia Britannica and Classic Writers volumes, pictures and old school books. He never did. He never inquired how we were going to live, or promise to send money for our support.

I had usually timed my vacation with my kids for the two weeks between Christmas and Three Kings Day to spend with family in Texas. Since all factories and schools in PR close those two weeks it made sense. This time I told everyone I was going to spend a few summer weeks in Texas to give my children some English summer courses and experience summer camp. While my children were supportive of our leaving their Dad, my son felt he needed to improve his English. I had consulted with his pediatrician who agreed with me that the issue was a simple release of the tissue beneath the tongue. It extended almost to the tip of the tongue. We took care of that and it was making a difference already.

The harder reality: I was going to look at the job market in Houston and in Corpus, especially with the two hospitals that I had trained and worked at. I was somewhat uncertain how future hospital employers would look at my education and successful career in nursing, but no recent experience in nursing. Or would prospective electronic industry employers see that I had recent electronic manufacturing and business experience but not the degrees? Would they think, "What was she thinking?" I could survive for two to three months financially while I found a job, which would make it easier to qualify for a loan to buy a house. I was certain that my parents would let us stay with them but their house was small. The three of us would have to stay in one small room.

But God was faithful to His promise, that I would not be alone. The Controller I had hired took me to lunch one day before I left and somehow he knew I was not coming back. He made some small talk, and then he said, "Belza, I looked at the books, and you have a lot of vacation and sick leave that you never took. That's worth almost four thousand bucks you probably will need." He handed me the check and just looked at me, almost in tears. I realized my husband must have told him, or he might have overheard me making one way reservations for our flight to Texas, to Houston, not Corpus. He must also be wondering what was going to happen to him. I had told him when I hired him that I would show him everything I did, in case something happened to me that I could not work, even for a couple of weeks. We had tested his ability to do that for a month, but I was still present.

I told him the truth, and that if worse came worse and I did not find a job, I would return to PR and just get a divorce, knowing my previous boss would hire me in some capacity at the hospital. He seemed to take hope on that, but insisted that I take the check. He also suggested that I hire a private detective to find out what my husband was up to. I said it did not matter to me what he was up to. I just knew he was not meeting my needs or my kids' needs as husband and father, and that our marriage had never been good. I told him about my spiritual and cultural struggles. I asked him to please not let the employees or stockholders know I might not come back. The success of the company was important to me. It was insurance for the future of my children. I told him I had chosen to hire him to ensure that. He seemed reassured.

I did not tell him that I had another possibility, just in case. I had also worked on Saturdays with a travel agency, handling the tourists who came to PR to start their seven day cruises of the Caribbean islands and had a whole day in PR before their ship sailed out at midnight. I had taken that job just to break my tension with my husband, but also to have some contact with people that were not employees or stockholders.

I was allowed to bring my children and I had enrolled them in pool scuba diving lessons. They had out of the blue offered me a full time job.

God Opens Doors

When I returned to Texas, by God's grace, doors opened for me to forge a new career and to grow my faith. Before going to Corpus, we flew into Houston, where my nephews were living, going to school and working. I missed them and knew they would be supportive of me no matter what. Maybe, if I found a job there, I would stay there. I wrote my resume and they reviewed it. They said I was not giving myself enough credit for the formation and management of the company and I re-wrote it. I distributed it to about twenty possible employers in Houston. My nephews asked me to leave a few copies to give to their numerous contacts. They drove me and the kids to Corpus. Half an hour before we got there, my whole body started to shake, not my bones, just my muscles. Nash pulled up to a cantina and bought me a stiff scotch and water to calm me down.

Once I got to my parents' house in Corpus, conscious to increase my children's proficiency in speaking and being instructed in English, I enrolled them in summer school. I was also conscious that a public school atmosphere would be different to the smaller class structure of their private school in PR. My sister-in-law drove me around wherever I needed to go or picked up the kids from school. Within a couple of weeks, the principal of summer instruction called me to ask me why I had enrolled them. All the diagnostics they had done, showed no need for remedial courses, which was the purpose of summer school at the middle school level. I explained our situation: that their instruction had been in a private school, in Spanish with English as an ESL course. I really needed them to stay in school due to the situation at my parents' home and my job search. He laughed and said my son had already fixed their projector and itching to work on their audio system. My daughter was helping the teacher with the other students. No problem, good luck with your job search.

I bought a car at auction with my brothers ensuring I got a good car for my money so I could continue with my job search. If my parents wondered why I was searching for a job, they never questioned me. By God's mercy, two executives who had been at my training hospital, were now higher up at the public hospital. I had been a Candy Striper and done pediatric and psychiatric internships there and other people knew me as well. Both executives told me I needed to re-write my resume, that even if I had not changed in the last thirteen years, they were certain I could run any department in the hospital! They would let me know in a few days, but were going to look at some possibilities. Unwittingly, they said this in front of my future boss, so that created some tension between us throughout my employment.

By God's mercy, TRW, the only electronic manufacturing employer in town had an opening for a Purchasing Expediter for their largest contract. The job was advertised at $7,000 less than what they offered me as a starting salary! Both hospitals offered me a job in new positions they had been thinking of creating and expedited their decision making, knowing I was available. Both were in the Human Resources Department. I negotiated my salary with all three and finally accepted the one with the public hospital. I would still be underemployed and underpaid, but thankful to God.

I qualified to buy a house on my own, only to be notified at the last minute by my bank, that they realized I was still married, and Texas being a Community Property state I had to wait until they qualified my husband as well. The other alternative they gave me was more acceptable to me and less problematic, I thought. I could get him to sign a notarized and witnessed affidavit that he had no claim on any property I acquired in Texas. I sent it off. He had not objected to getting requests for references from the three employers who wanted to hire me, but he blew his stack at the audacity of me getting a home. "What the h—- are you going to do with a house in six months when you come back?"

I had actually dismissed and/or forgotten his request for "six months to be free." It took me a few seconds to answer, "Oh, that's right, you asked for six months to be free. Well, I am granting you six months plus the rest of your life to be free. Did you really think I would put my life on a shelf for six months, disrupt the children's lives again, and return to the farce of a life we've been living?" I hung up after a few seconds of silence. I felt strangely at peace and also had a feeling of anticipation. I actually had closed a door that set me free.

The Holy Spirit Changes My Path

After two years with the Public Hospital, I got a call from the Director of HR at my Catholic Training Hospital. They were creating a new position as Employment Manager for Nursing Personnel and he said that "I was made for it." He still had my resume. As it was, I had succeeded in filling the almost 300 nursing personnel vacancies at the public hospital, plus the Employee Health Program Alice and I had developed was running well. It was saving the hospital money with the Health Risk Assessment questionnaire we had developed, with the input from clinicians. It reduced the number and extent of tests and exams needed for new hires and even new patients that entered the public assistance clinic program.

The tension with my boss was impacting my ability to do my job. Examples: she delayed approving the travel expenses for out of town interviews for management applicants or for the light snacks and beverages for receptions we held for Nursing School Graduates. I had to cancel a couple of things. Another example of this was in my first performance review. I had asked for the possibility of having separate offices for me and Alice, the RN I supervised for the Employee Health Program we were developing. It was awkward for me to interview new recruits, and for her to do the Health Risk Assessments, which were very personal, with both of us experiencing interruptions with phone calls and walk ins. In my review, "Belza seems to have a special need to work without interruptions."

The position with my training Hospital, offered only slightly more money but seemed like a good next step in this new career. The travel involved with Nurse Recruitment was creating a problem for me, with my children who refused a babysitter, (though I called it a house sitter) because they were 13 and 11. Sometimes I drove or I flew out on the red-eye special and came back at 10 or 11 at night if it was a one day job fair nearby. True, they did not need a babysitter, but as adolescents they needed supervision. It seemed like a God-sent offer to me. I had postponed my studies because though I still managed to pass, I would probably get a diploma without any "honor".

In the interview in April (1980), I informed them that I had scheduled surgery for early June so that it would not interfere with all the nursing school graduations, receptions and job fairs around the end of May. My current boss had agreed to the sick leave and I had enough days accumulated for the convalescing period. They had no problem waiting for a mid-July start date. When I accepted the position and presented my resignation, my boss also agreed that my sick leave would serve as required notice.

When I had told my parents that I had gotten a better paying job, starting after surgery, Papa said, "Why have you had so many jobs, mi'ja? Look at your brothers, they've been in the same job for years and will retire from it twenty years from now."

Well, not much had changed since they had told me I'd had too many boyfriends (two). But then again I had not stopped "being different", going against the cultural current. However, now I was just more mature and forgiving, a bit more perceptive to the love behind their concern. More importantly, I was more comfortable with myself, with being "different". I explained the situation I had with traveling and the need to supervise the kids, and he nodded in understanding.

With my new job, the first and urgent assignment was to arrange a nurse recruitment trip to the Philippines. Within thirty days I had all the visas, passports, and Philippine Embassy authorization documents required for our purpose. I also made personal plans for family members to stay with my children the entire 21 days I would be gone and executed a limited power of attorney.

A Filipino nursing supervisor would precede us by a week to arrange interview rooms at the hotel and some media exposure for the 20 days we would be there. The Director of Nursing (DON) would accompany me on the flight. They would do the interviews, and I would do the required dealings with the Labor Department and then deal with the offer letter for the nurses approved by them, explain our benefits, the assistance we would provide and get all the information and personal documents I needed for their H1B visas before we left. I had reserved a rental car, which luckily was pending my experiencing a taxi cab/jitney ride view of traffic before finalizing. I opted out.

Once settled at the hotel and at the interview room, with copying equipment and phones, my companions started interviewing. I took a jitney to the Ministry of Labor building to present my documents to the Minister of Labor as instructed by the Embassy. Upon arrival I was directed to a room and met by two Philippine Recruitment Agency reps. I told them I was the recruiter and did not need their services. Before I left I made another appointment with the Minister of Labor for the next day. Same thing happened again twice. In the meantime the interviews continued and the Hotel kept changing the Marquee announcement for our "event". That's better for you." the front desk explained.

I asked them how I could make contact with the U. S. Embassy in Manila, they said "Good.", and even offered to have the hotel take me there once I had an appointment. I told them I was going today, with or without a firm appointment. Once again they said "Good." I called and got an in with an Aide to the Ambassador (Sandman, I think). First thing he asked was, "Why should I help you, my job is to keep people from going to the US." Finding out that he was from Minnesota, where I had lived with the Red Cross job and a few months after my marriage, I explained the severe shortage of nurses in the US , resorting to two year schools graduating unskilled nurses, and statistics in his state (yes, he had an elderly mother and family there, he said.) I said that is why he would help me, besides that I was a US citizen seeking help on foreign soil. He made an appointment for me with the Ambassador for an hour from then.

Mr. Ambassador (Mr. M?) turned white when I explained my mission and the trouble I was having turning in my authorizing documents from the Houston Filipino Embassy and finding out that yes, we were holding the interviews and yes, we'd had hundreds of nurses show up. He made two calls, one with the Minister of Labor and one to the hotel manager. Then he said "Young lady, you are lucky you didn't start an international incident." He explained that the Philippine government is the only authorized exporter of labor, and it is done with government to government agreements. Also, that although Marshall Law had just been lifted, it was prohibited for more than three people to assemble. I showed him the documents and instructions I'd gotten from the Houston Philippine Embassy and said, "Then why are they misrepresenting and misinforming people? Are these documents toilet paper?"

He picked up the phone again and asked me to step out. Then he came out and asked how soon I could get to the Minister's office. I said I'd see if the hotel car was still waiting for me, if not I had seen many jitneys lined up outside the gates. He said he would get a car to take me to the Labor Ministry, wait to take me back to the hotel, and he would take care of dismissing the hotel's car, said the Minister was waiting for me. It dawned on me why the hotel manager had said "Good." And why they kept changing the name of our "event" on the Marquee. Obvious too was that they were consciousness of assisting their own to get better paying jobs in the US. This was a long time ago, remember.

At the Ministry I was ushered in right away and the Minister actually tried to talk me into using the Recruitment Agencies. I explained that my employer had assigned me, and I would not incur unnecessary expenses for them with recruitment agency fee as high as they were to the employer and to each nurse. I had done due diligence in inquiring from the Filipino Consulate what the requirements were and obtaining authorizing documents they said I needed, and frankly, at many points in my preparation I had asked of them if there was anyone else I needed to contact or anything else I needed to do. They could have informed me correctly.

I said I had contacted Filipino recruitment agencies in Texas and they had explained prohibitive costs to the hospital and to the nurse. These nurses' families had already sold their last caribou to put the most promising child through school and that the agency fees to them would just add to their burden, and to the nurse when they needed to concentrate on learning English, passing the State Boards, adjust to a new job and new country. Also, I would not be doing my job in directly selecting employees for the DON to consider and for our hospital. No, not acceptable.

Finally, he asked me to wait outside his office a few minutes. Shortly he called me in and a couple of lawyers came in with a sample contract and a stenographer, I had to make a call to my employer to fax authorization to negotiate, (I was still in my three-month probationary period) and to sign a contract, and we spent the rest of the afternoon and into the evening discussing clause by clause, and finally we had a contract. At some point someone discreetly brought in a tray with coffee, soft drinks, finger foods and sweet *encaimadas*. I had not eaten since an early breakfast but was embarrassed to help myself. The two lawyers and stenographer dug in and signaled me to join in.

They said the Minister himself would have to sign with me. I said I would come back in the morning as soon as he came in, and they said he was still there. He came in and said "my lawyers say you're a tough lawyer and negotiator". I informed him I was not a lawyer, but did know the laws I had to comply with in my job.

He said "Young lady, you just negotiated the first ever and hopefully the last, **Government to Private Employer Agreement** to export nurses. You should be very proud." Frankly, I found the term "export nurses" offensive, and did not immediately grasp the enormity of that accomplishment, but I thanked him. I told him he should see the opportunity the shortage of nurses and physical therapists the US was experiencing as an opportunity for more similar contracts. When he looked puzzled, I said tactfully,

"I would see it as an opportunity to establish schools equivalent to the ones in the US and even language training to help your people." (The thought crossed my mind, "Here you are suggesting solutions to problems to someone with such a prestigious position.) Thankfully he did not take offense and he said he wished he could find employees as resourceful and caring as I was. He said, "You wouldn't happen to be available, would you?" We both laughed.

Silently, I thanked the Holy Spirit for guiding me, helping me make quick recall of our employee benefits, so that we'd be consistent and fair to all our employees Their contract went beyond our benefits and I had to say we could not agree, because we'd have to offer our employees the same and that would be too expensive. I thanked Him for putting words in my mouth to be tactful and come up with alternatives.

Belza, Juliet (Beth's Aunt), Beth and DON in the Philippines

We hired 38 nurses, who arrived in groups, as I had arranged, so that we could give special attention to them when they came. I was very empathetic and intuitive, since I'd had such a hard time with my nursing license in PR and with learning the culture. In addition to having a special program to orient them to the hospital, I added a day on acculturation, their rights and responsibilities as H1B Visa employees, their visa held by the Hospital, and all that that implied. I accompanied them on one apartment hunting trip, a group visit to a grocery store with a bunch of "special" ads and leaflets, and to a bank. The nurses were required to send back money and start an account with a family member authorized to sign. I had said we would set up a payroll deduction and direct deposit to the nurses' US bank and they could authorize electronic transfers to comply with the requirement.

I consulted a Filipino priest that Beth, the Nursing Supervisor who had gone to the Philippines with me, had introduced to me. I felt they would need spiritual support from someone who knew their culture. He agreed to meet with me close to 5 P.M. and I explained to him what I was doing to help the nurses and what help I needed from him. He thought it was great that I would go that far, not too many employers would, etc. I thought I would briefly tell him why I had a special kinship with them and my own experience in PR. I wanted the nurses to succeed I said. Plus this was a Catholic Hospital, which make it easier to justify paid time for employees to get spiritual conferences as part of their orientation.

Somehow, I must have slipped to talking about my situation in PR and wishing I'd had a priest who made himself available to his parishioners. I did not pay attention to his movement when he put his stole on, (to hear confessions), until he was absolving me of all my sins. After two years of encouragement from the nurse that had helped me at the other hospital set up the Employee Health Program, to forgive myself because Jesus had already forgiven me and do Reconciliation (Confess), so I could start receiving the Eucharist, I still had not done it. It had been that simple to do it now. I knew he was the right person to meet and understood why I had called him. The Holy Spirit's hand imprint was clear to read.

On the other hand, I was really, I'll call it "disappointed", but still proud to learn on the Spohntaneous monthly bulletin that the recruitment trip to the Philippines had been named the Corporate Achievement of the Year (Corporate! That meant for all the US and international hospitals, schools and universities the order of nuns held!) and that the Director of Nurses had proudly accepted the commemorative trophy at the annual banquet held at The Plush Hotel, at Headquarter City. (Too much pride for the Filipino Supervisor and this "Mexican" who had done all the preparation to handle?) The DON had boarded the plane and asked, "What do I have to do?", and I had handed her a folder, with all she needed to do. Attached also was a script for a scheduled radio interview we had when we got there, her itinerary and return ticket. Who had had to think on her feet to handle the obstacles faced and not give up, which would have made the trip a waste? I did get a note from the HR Director with the authorization to sign a contract on behalf of the hospital, "Congratulations, you have approved your probationary period. Will discuss an increase when you return."

I had already gotten my award when I received the Eucharist after fifteen years of silent tears in Mass. I would be further rewarded twenty years later when I visited my sister at the hospital, after her surgery, and saw one of the nurses we had hired. She recognized me, hugged me, and told me thirty-two of them were still there, citizens, and some were even supervisors or head nurses. Some had gotten Masters Degrees and specialization certifications. Over the next few days I would get to see and get up to date with a few more of them, who had heard I was sitting with my sister. Thank you Jesus, thank you Santi Espiritu.

Reflections:

1. Have I ever had to navigate in uncharted waters? Why did I persist or give up? Did I recognize a higher purpose for pursuing?

2. Who helped me? Did the angels who helped see a higher purpose?

3. If someone else was solely recognized for a team effort, would I see that the person also deserved credit and not be resentful of her? Would I give up trying to do a good job?

I Built the Path By Walking*

Having made my Reconciliation and started to take the Eucharist, I realized the Church was completely different now, post Vatican II. The mission of Vatican II, was to take our church back to the basics, which meant giving lay people expanded roles and involvement, restoring the Rites for Christian initiation for Adults (RCIA) and promoting formation of small groups or Small Christian Communities to read scripture, reflect on the Word and live out its message in our everyday life. RCIA and faith formation had a focus or reconverting "separated brethren" and bringing them back. *Dear God, did you do all this for ME?*

I embraced it all with a passion and found a loving God, a faith that requires mindful discernment of what God, Christ and the Holy Spirit are calling me to do, and to be every day, in every way. I realized that all along, in mapping all aspects of my life, and in the decision making process of pursuing that plan, I never had asked God what he wanted of or for me. I thanked Him after things went my way! If they didn't, I worked harder to make them happen. How arrogant and naïve of me that I asked him for signs that I was doing the right thing but never paused to listen to Him tell me if I was on the right path, according to His Plan for me.

God not only opened doors to help me survive economically but he also put angels that understood the quest I had undertaken and invited me to retreats and parish based studies. Eventually I got involved with Small Christian Communities. They opened my eyes to experience Christ and Church in a way beyond any of my dreams, with others who became my Brothers and Sisters in Christ.

I have no regrets. When you fall, you become humble and realize that you are not so perfect, that you are capable of sin. You can let God do His good in you and get up. This period in my life strengthened and matured me as a wiser person of faith. I could survive in the street of life, and be more vigilant of not losing my salvation. The past forty-two years, I have been on an incredible journey spiritually, career-wise and personally. I have a son and a daughter, four grandchildren, and soon will have a great grandchild. My SCCs members are my extended family. I hold on to friendships I have made through the years and in many places. All glory and praise to God and the Angels who helped me along the way.

God Protects His Own

In 1981, I borrowed money go to Puerto Rico to a stockholders meeting of the company. I got the notice, which was an exact copy of the one I would send out every year, but after not getting a notice in the last two years, I wondered what was going on. This was an opportunity to find out what was happening with the Company, and to try to get a property and divorce settlement. I called a lawyer in PR, the nephew Sister C. had referred me to, set a meeting with my husband and his lawyer. I am sure now that Sister asked him to help me pro bono, for I never got a bill from him and he never filed for the divorce. In reality, I was not interested in getting the divorce as much as getting what was rightfully my children's, to make a better life for them. I would also ensure that my absence did not set the company back. A meeting was set for a day after the stockholders meeting.

Praise God I had a good paying job, however, things were tight, as I had to start my life anew buying a house, furniture, car, winter clothing for the three of us and more. The children were growing by leaps and bounds, they needed braces, and they were active, had minor accidents, and needed instruments for band, equipment for sports. When I'd had surgery in 1980 between jobs, I ended up exhausting my paid leave, and because of a budget glitch in the approval by the board of the salary, I'd had about three weeks without a salary. This had set me back, and I needed the settlement to catch up, start saving for the kids' college.

I had heard that the company in Puerto Rico was not doing well, with a lawsuit about a driver having an accident in a company van, while under the influence, and a supervisor starting a competing business. My husband had hired the driver at a bar! The supervisor had explained to me by letter that since I had left, things were not the same. Some stockholders had pulled out their stock when they realized I had left for good. (All stockholders were friends or former co-workers of my husband, since he had wanted nothing to do with my hospital co-workers and friends.) I wanted the company to survive, which is why I had trained a controller and another assistant before I left. I planned on transferring my stock to my children, with a voting proxy to my husband. This would enable him to make and execute decisions. The company actually lasted for 12 years after I left, but never grew.

The contracts I'd negotiated, were renewed without renegotiation for more advantageous terms or larger work orders. No new contracts had been acquired.

At the meeting, I got emotional and discouraged because his lawyer was the sister of the supervisor who had left and we had all been good friends. She was of course going for my jugular, doing her job for her client. She said I had abandoned my marriage and the company, even though he had "only wanted a six month separation". My lawyer did not seem to have the same vigor and information for defending my interests and I did not have the heart to expose all the humiliating background. I had never felt so alone.

I braced myself to keep from crying by putting my fists in the pockets of a jacket I was wearing. I touched a square of paper and was surprised for I had sent the jacket to the cleaners before the trip. It was like the tightly folded notes that boys and girls used to send each other through friends in middle school.

I pulled it out, opened it and Mama Panchita's handwriting jumped out at me. It was a prayer for my success because it was the just thing for me and my children to get what was rightfully ours, and paraphrased similar Psalms in the Lamentations group. She wrote in Spanish! Of course, I broke down crying. With everyone staring at me, I handed the note to my lawyer and just said "Mi Mama." He read it, called for a recess till the next day. I asked him to stay so I could give him information he needed.

He came back with much greater passion. We did come to a fair agreement, worth $278 K in assets, plus child support, but its execution never happened and that was beyond his control. I realized that I was the only one acting in good faith and that I would never receive a penny. My husband got a judge to put an injunction on the settlement, claiming he had to terminate all the employees in order to pay me. What I regret losing, emotionally, is the Encyclopedia Britannica set, which ended up being eaten by termites. Everything I had packed before I left, pictures, books, materials I had used for my sewing, all was fodder for the termites. He told the judge that I expected him to ship old books, which would cost a fortune to ship.

We did not get a divorce until after my daughter got married in 1997, at the command of my children to their dad. At that time I had substantial assets and salary and they felt he might develop an interest in them, since he was not doing well. They had paid for his flight for her wedding. I gave my son money to buy him a suit and new shoes to wear for the wedding. I have a one paragraph divorce decree: uncontested divorce for long term abandonment, no minor children or assets to contest. My peace of mind, family and faith untouched by any earthly court.

To this day I have no idea how Mama put that note in my jacket, how she knew that was what I would wear and would need her prayers so very much. I had packed at home, met my sister-in-law at Mama's home, transferred my suitcase to her car and we went to the airport. But I never saw Mama get out of the house.

When I came back, I asked her how she had put the note in the pocket of my jacket. I told her all about what had happened and thanked her. All she said *"Dios defiende los suyos."* God defends His own. I can add "and the Holy Spirit helps Him."

Reflection:

1. Do I see God's hand in inexplicable things that happen in my life?

2. Do I rebel at God at the loss of material things?

3. Do I weigh material loss against leaving a dehumanizing situation that separates me from God? Do I trust that God will help me and that He will welcome me back with open arms?

6

BUMPS IN MY LIFE–HEALING JOURNEYS GOD PLANNED

Uninvited Invader

The number on the caller ID was all too familiar. I prayed as I answered. When the surgeon himself said, "Hello, Mrs. Ramos." My mouth dried up and I could barely talk. "Please come to my office tomorrow. Bring a close family member."

My heart stopped beating, my ears buzzed and I started hyperventilating. I knelt in prayer or my knees just buckled.

My son, my son-in-law, my grandson on his lap, and I met with the doctor. He outlined treatment options with their increased probability that the cancer would not return.

"Mom, go with the most aggressive option." To this day they believe *they* convinced me, but actually it was my grandson who abruptly stopped playing with the Surgeon's paperweight and held out his arms to me. A few weeks back, I had been playing "airplane" with him, when his little heel touched the bump in my breast. I tell him he saved my life.

"Is the recovery time longer if I have reconstruction at the same time?"

"No, it's six weeks either way."

"Then let's do it by August 15, because I am going to Portugal, Spain and France on September 30. I paid for this pilgrimage over a year ago.

We'll even see the Basque region where my ancestors probably come from! I can start the chemo when I return."

This was July 28, 2002! "Mrs. Ramos, getting the plastic surgeon, the anesthesiologist and myself plus an open operating room concurrently available may take up to a month. Let's wait until you come back; you'd enjoy yourself more."

"No way. I refuse to take this unwelcome stowaway on my trip."

Seeing my resolve, he said, "You know, let me see what I can do." Back home, I activated my prayer brigade to pray for: surgery by August 15, a good outcome, and quick healing. Prayer answered, I stopped at St. Brigid's for a blessing, on my way to the hospital, I but the church was closed for the Assumption of Blessed Virgin Mary on August 15. That was okay: She **would** be with me regardless.

My Grandson Nehemiah and I

Portugal, Spain and France

I flew to Europe Sept 30, with an admonition to take it easy. I "failed" to tell my surgeons we were advised to wear comfortable walking shoes, as we'd be walking an average of 6 miles each 12-14 hour day. I had healed well except for about an inch on my abdominal incision.

This trip had a primary and a secondary purpose. The primary purpose was what a pilgrimage is all about: encountering Christ in all aspects. The secondary purpose formed in my mind as I was preparing for it and anticipating it, as well as the Italy trip later. I had been to Spain, France and Italy and several other countries in Europe and Scandinavia and my husband and I had fought all throughout. It was a business trip for him and I was to arrange dinners for the executives of companies that his employer did business with. I would do that at the hotels we were staying, then sign up for tours the rest of the day while he had meetings. The fights ensued if I got compliments for the choice of menu and wines, etc. or because I managed to get by in their language with my Spanish in Italy and a smattering of French I had learned hoping to get into the Peace Corp or the International–ARC, or especially if they complimented me on my looks or outfits. Goodness, they were business men and their wives, probably just doing business. I mindfully determined and asked God's help to make new, happier and more peaceful memories and to forgive on this trip.

The trip was every bit what I expected. I encountered Jesus Christ in the Holy Sites, bonded with my fellow pilgrims, I also received signs that gave me hope. In Portugal, at Fatima, a great niece of Lucia Santos was at the well drawing water for pilgrims. How special! At the procession when the Rosary was said in different languages, by thousands of pilgrims bearing candles, I actually heard my mother's voice, who had a deep devotion to Mary and the rosary saying *"Dichosos ojos, Mi'ja."* She knew my eyes and ears were overjoyed as my memories of our family rosaries came to life.

In Spain at Santiago de Campostella, a Spanish Missal was placed on the altar for our priest for daily Mass. He asked me to stand by him and translate a few lines of each part of the Mass to prompt his memory. That is my most memorable Mass: front row witness to the exact moment when the bread and wine transubstantiate to the body and blood of Christ!

Unfortunately, the minor inconvenience of changing a small dressing became a major one, because apparently I'm allergic to adhesive. By the time we got to France, I was miserable with a larger area reacting to the tape. Yet I climbed over 360 stone steps to the top of Mont San Michel, and toured the Benedictine Abbey.

Taking the healing bath at Lourdes was my singular goal but the baths were closed when we arrived until the morning we planned to leave! A group of us, with the tour director, got to the baths at 4:30 AM, but over 200 people were already ahead of us. I asked the director if we would leave without doing the baths. She looked at me with divine understanding and love and said "You know, they won't leave without me; let's pray we don't hold them up too long." I started crying. She always stuck strictly to every timeline.

Finally, wearing only a tunic, the attendants asked me to make my petition before dunking me in freezing spring water. Dressing quickly, we sprinted uphill to the waiting bus. Two hours later we stopped for lunch and I went to change my dressing; it was absolutely clean! I was totally healed! Awed and humbled that Jesus and Mary deemed me, a sinner, worthy of this miracle, I shared it with the group that evening.

Our Lady of Lourdes

Of course this small miracle, made my first pilgrimage indelible in my memory. I chose this group because people at Holy Trinity remembered the tour director and her husband when they had been members of the parish. Fred had been a Deacon for several years and Loreen, his wife, had a travel agency and was a Tour Director to Holy Sites. They had recently moved to Tennessee. The Spiritual Director, Fr. Gail had recently retired from our parish. Of course, my friend Delia asked me to be her roommate and several other parishioners that I knew signed up. But we have all been to retreats, vacations and even professional seminars, where we are inspired, enlightened and lit on fire, but shortly forget the feelings and even details when it's over. Even with these personal connections to make it special, other features can help us stay "on the mountain" longer and recall the details as well. These are:

+ Follow the tour director's suggestions for comfortable dress and shoes. Often they will give you tips for staying safe, avoiding pickpockets, and establishing a buddy system so no one gets left behind.

+ Begin training by walking as soon as you book. Lose a few pounds if needed. Often you will walk an average of 6-8 miles, visiting at least two sites a day.

+ Provide yourself even a modest budget to buy at least one memorable souvenir, typical of the site or of the country. Examples: I bought a handmade Mantilla in Spain, a Murano glass necklace and vase in Italy, Loaves and Fishes tray and butter plates in the Holy Land.

+ Take lots of pictures, develop them soon upon return, and make the most memorable ones your PC screen saver. A journal or notes also help. Offer your family to show them at a specific date and place, Email them from your hotel computer room or your device.

+ Consciously decide to get to know all or most of your fellow pilgrims. Rotate where you sit on the bus, for meals and daily Mass.

+ Be aware that your objective is to have an encounter with Jesus, be it at the Holy Sites (obviously), but also with your fellow pilgrims, the beauty and unique atmosphere of the country, people who serve you and cities you visit.

✦ Notice the bonding that occurs among the group and leaders.

✦ Pluses: The tour director provides quiet time at each site, maybe reading the scriptures about the specific event or at the site where Jesus made it happen. Bible reading will never be the same for you.

✦ Time for sharing among the group, even if it is in the bus, but better if it is in a private room after dinner at the hotel.

✦ Last but not least: daily mass and a spiritual director who is available for private sessions.

Italy – The Vatican

My fellow pilgrims to Spain, Portugal and France joined my prayer brigade for the next bump ahead. I had also signed up for a pilgrimage to Italy in 2004. Guess what? I was diagnosed with colon cancer eight weeks before that trip. This time I did not panic, certain that God was planning these healing journeys for me. This one would start five weeks after surgery! From diagnosis to surgery I felt like I was in good hands. The Gastroenterologist, who found the cancerous polyp and I share the same three letters on our name and last name. The surgeon she referred me to, was Dr. Ramos. He is given credit for developing a surgical procedure to do an external colon resection, removing a six inch cancerous section, sewing the colon back up and reinserting the colon into the abdomen. All he needs are four small incisions on either side of the abdomen. This greatly reduces infection. God-incidences can set you at ease if you have faith.

"Wake up Belza, you are out of surgery and going to your room as soon as you are awake and stable. I believe you are cancer-free now and won't require follow-up chemo, but of course, I've sent all the tissue to the lab for tests, just to be sure."

At the Vatican our daily Mass was switched from St. Anne's Chapel to St. Peregrine's Chapel, patron saint of cancer victims. That was a huge sign that the surgeon's words after surgery would be true. Upon my return, Dr. Ramos called to tell me I was cancer free and hoped I'd had a wonderful trip. I told him about the switch of our daily Mass to St. Peregrine Chapel without explanation. He laughed and said, "Oh you already knew the results."

My roommate on this trip was my SCC sister in Christ, Delia. She and I bought some tiny Barbie luggage. Symbolically, we stuffed the luggage with all our "stuff" (resentments, bad decisions, etc. that we had carried around in our hearts and mind.) We threw our "black bags" into the Tiber River from one of the many bridges in Rome. Now I could have more joyous, peaceful memories of Rome and Italy.

I have been colon cancer-free for sixteen years. Never doubt in the power of prayer and that God helps us even before we know we need help.

Reflections

1. How do I view adversity (illnesses, personal and economic problems, etc.) in my life?

2. Do I rebel against God, drown in self-pity or blame others or realize that God is "refining me" like gold?

3. Do I offer my suffering up to God, put it on the Cross with Jesus' suffering, so that He can do the most good with it?

7

OUR DAILY BREAD – FAMILY HISTORY AND FAITH PASSED ON AT THE KITCHEN TABLE

Family Cookbook

When I read that Russian *"babushkas"*, Spanish and Mexican *"Abuelitas"*, German *Oma's* kept faith and family traditions alive and passed them on to their children and grandchildren in the preparation and sharing of meals, during wars and political upheavals and oppressive regimes, I wanted to be that grandmother. So with my oldest granddaughter, Brittany, who spent a week twice a year with us, I knew I had to come up with a way of having long lasting impact. We are a very large family, so although she met everyone it was hard for her to get to really know them. Tony took time off and he and Brittany would come to San Antonio, while she was in Texas. This way we could all be together with my daughter Renée and her family, while Brittany was with us.

When she came to visit the very first time, she was thirteen. My son and I, and in fact our whole family felt like we had to catch up for lost time. I had just returned from Italy and had all my souvenirs and gifts laid out to decide who got what so I could start distributing them. It was important to me that she know about our culture and history, different from her mother's side of the family. I was respectful of the difference in religions as well. She was curious about everything she saw laid out, but was attracted to the crystal rosary I had bought at the Vatican gift store for myself. She asked me for it. My only concern was that she understand what it was, what it meant, and that her mother would not object to her having it. We had a conversation about that and she promised to return it to me if her mother objected. She still has it.

She also responded to my Mexican, Tex-Mex, and Spanish cooking, reporting back to her mother how I made the best this or that. On one of her visits she surprised me standing beside me making potato and eggs for breakfast tacos. She asked, "When do you know the potatoes are ready?"

I said, "When they are translucent," showing her some that had a white center and translucent edges, and some that were fully cooked. "That is why you slice the potatoes fairly uniform, so they cook pretty much at the same time. You stir them around to help that. Mama Panchita told me that she stirred love and blessings on us into the food!"

She loved a Trifle I made and asked how I had made it. I made it again before she left and she watched. I told her the layered Trifle was like people: all different flavors, textures, colors that when blended together make a rich dessert. Each layer enhances the total.

Mama Panchita, would always say the bonds of family are sacred: much is forgiven with family love. The family talking at the dinner table to plan, solve issues, or raise up a family member who is down, and give thanks to God, builds strong bonds. When you marry, you marry into your spouse's whole family, the parents become *co-madres* and *com-padres*, co-mothers and fathers. The families blend and thus community is built. Make your own memories and pass them on to your children and your children's children, just like our genes are passed on to them. I am grateful to Brittany and Joe, because they are involving my family in every step of their pregnancy with my great granddaughter.

I thought of making a family cookbook for her when she became engaged. We met Joe before they got married, having both of them come to Texas during one of her visits. It was my wedding gift to Brittany and Joe. I got to meet both their families and I just love Joe's grandmother. They all thought the cookbook was the most unique wedding present they had ever seen. They loved how personal it is, with the stories that go with each recipe.

Brittany and Joe

Omelet of *Nopalitos*, Faith and Love

Nopalitos are a traditional Lenten staple. You can use them for breakfast, lunch or dinner dishes with any meat, as a side dish without meat and/or in a flour tortilla as a taco. As a child, my mother would tell me that *nopalitos, capirotada y albóndigas de salmon* are "Lenten foods".

In the preparation of food and in sharing it with family and friends, *Mamacitas, abuelitas y tías* pass on traditions, faith, family history and customs from generation to generation. Manners and proper behavior for *Señoritas y verdaderas mujeres* are worked in at every chance, especially during the *sobre mesa,* when families serve desert and coffee and linger for family talk, closing with prayers.

I liked going with Mama to the garden or brush to gather fresh ingredients for our dishes. I observed as she prepared them for canning. I wondered how she knew exactly how many jars to keep for our family after she gave away some to neighbors, "who have come up on hard times". She also saved a few to barter with.

"Vamos, mi'ja, vamos a cortar nopalitos". As the youngest child, it was seldom I had her all to myself. She helped me put on my *gorro,* and with a knife and a pan we made our way to the brush behind our house. I knew that strip of brush like the palm of hand, every exotic species of cactus like *maguey, chayote, peyote, and salvia, aloe vera and drago,* and every bird, its nest and eggs, for I had unlimited exploring rights.

I thought as we walked, *my dad lets me hang around also, when he burns off the thorns from the cactus planks to feed to the horses and cow. He wears leather gloves to protect his hands from the thorns, as he holds the planks with the pitchfork over the fire.*

Mama and I don't have gloves. I ask her, "Mama, why do we eat *nopal*? That's what the horses and cows eat and it has *espinas!* We don't even have gloves on." Immediately, I regretted asking. She might think I was telling her what to do and never invite me again.

"Ay no, mija, ya veras. Animals eat old cactus. I'll show you how we clean these". She handed me the pan and I followed her holding the pan just below her hands to catch the *nopalitos.* We were dancing around the cactus.

"Mama, they're heavy."

"*Ya mero, mi'ja,* we almost have enough."

"The heat is coming right through my shoes and my *gorro,* Mama." *Ay,* there I was complaining again! But she did not get angry with me.

As we walked back home she continued teaching me about fasting. We fast and abstain from meat during Lent because *Jesucristo* fasted for forty days in the desert. It cleanses our bodies, which are a temple for our souls and *Diosito* can come into our clean hearts. *Limpio de pecado y limpio de impurezas".*

Once we got home she started cleaning the *penquitas,* dicing them into strips, soaking them in boiled water with *vinagre,* to cut the slime. She talked as she worked, explaining what she was doing. I half heard her, because when I became a nurse I would live in a city. *Nopalitos* don't grow in the city. No one eats them in the city.

She put them in sterile Mason Jars and sealed the jars with melted wax. Then she put the sterile lids on. She stacked the jars in the pantry upside down.

I asked, really explained, "Do you turn the jars upside down because air would be sucked into the jars if they were upright as the nopalitos cool? Then they'd spoil? Cool air takes up less space than hot air."

She looked at me a long while, processing what I'd said, laughed, "*Ay Mi'ja*, I just do it because that's what Mama Cecilia did," then she thought a while and said quietly, "but you're right. That's what happens."

We would have Omelet de *nopalitos* at breakfast, *ensalada de nopalitos con* tuna or *catan* for lunch and *nopalitos guisados* for dinner all through Lent.

Blooming Cactus plant

Calabazita con Pollo y Elote

My oldest sister Carmen cooked like the *verdaderas mujeres* according to our mother's criteria. "Real women" do not need a recipe, they just add a pinch of this and a handful of that." I wanted to develop the recipes for dishes from my mother's table, so I asked Carmen to put her "handful" or "pinch" into a bowl or measuring spoon so I'd have a measure. Mama would also mention a name as she put a "pinch" or drop, a potato quarter. "Uno para Luis, uno para Belzita, etc. I also incorporate valuable tips on the preparation of the ingredients and the cooking in my recipes, i.e. don't stir *Calabaza con Pollo* while it cooks because it gets mushy.

As the kitchen filled with aromas of sweet, starchy *elote*; pungent cumin and spices; the Calabaza – the earth after a fresh rain, Carmen shared her memories of our family before I was born. The ingredients stirred up stories.

My Itchy Birth

She told me that Mama Panchita had been shucking ears of corn and getting rid of the silk strands and chaff in the wind, when she went into labor with me. She sent one of my brothers to bring the mid-wife and while she waited she made a big pot of *Calabaza* **con Pollo y Elote** for the family **and** boiled water to sterilize the birthing instruments. Since I was the twelfth child, I came rather fast and Mama did not have time to draw water from the cistern and bathe. She went through labor covered with chaff. That made me itch!! Carmen and I added current memories also. Most days we packed up what we cooked and took it to share with our nephew Nash who was a patient at the VA hospital and with any lucky staff that came into his room. Having grown up with me, he and I had our own set of memories about fresh corn.

No Mas Elote, Toto

"I remember how when it came time to harvest the corn, we would have *elote con todo* for weeks. Corn in scrambled eggs*, crema de elote, and even pudding de elote.*"

"Oh, yes." I said. "One year, Toto (I slipped into calling Papa "Toto" after Nash and Eddie started calling him that.) took you to help him harvest *elote* at the ranch. You were so proud to go because for two years Toto had said you were too young. You and Toto came back to Salineño with a wagon load of *elotes* to deliver to his sisters, sell to the grocer and for our household. He wanted to just turn around to harvest the rest but you did not want to go back with him."

"*No más elote* for me, Toto."

Carmen laughed "I think we all said that and done that."

"You'd had enough *elote*. Then, when you realized that Mama Panchita was serving fresh corn fixed in different ways for breakfast, lunch and dinner, you figured you might as well have gone back to the ranch with Toto."

Yes, the important things don't change. I hope these stories will help Brittany and Joe know our family better. More importantly, I hope they pass them on to their children and grandchildren. Brittany and Joe are involving us in every step of the their pregnancy with my great granddaughter.

Nash on Hospital Pass, me and my grandson

A Real *Mujer…According To Mama (2010)*

A *molcajete* in her kitchen
To grind garlic, pepper and cumin.
A *palote and comal*
To make her own tortillas.

Quilting bees and tamaladas
She must organize
Sharing jokes and stories,
Faith and more, the prize.

Makes invisible hems,
Knits and tats,
Sews tiny even quilting stitches,
Darns holes and all that.

Home clean and orderly,
You can eat off her floors,
Clothes all washed
And folded in their drawers.

Her home a sacred space.
A crucifix over every doorway,
A blessing and a prayer,
Send her family on their way.

Her beauty is within,
Earrings she must wear,
Her clothing must cover
So no one stares.

These things I forget,
Downright ignore.
But I am a real *mujer*
At least most of the time.

8

ON PILGRIMAGE

Everyday Pilgrimages — Connecting

My whole life is a pilgrimage,
Seeking to encounter God in any of His divine persons.
Looking for places on earth which God himself visits,
Perhaps to be close with us, his beloved children.
Hoping to meet Him on an ordinary day,
Doing ordinary things, with an ordinary human.
Such encounters invoke the same sense of God's presence
I found far away in Sacred Sites and Holy Ground.

With memories of Fatima and Lourdes on my mind,
Slowly winding through the Pyrenees Mountains
Toward Spain's sacred sites,
I took in the breathtaking beauty round every bend.
Mountains dressed in myriad hues of green;
Tall majestic spruces, junipers and unnamed trees
Tickling low thick clouds in deep blue sky.
Sun casting purple shadows in deep crevices and valleys.
Utter silence only broken by rhythmic breathing
Of sleeping fellow pilgrims.

Sure that God would rush in with the wind,
Resisted a strong urge to open the bus window

And share the moment with another being.
None of the cathedrals we've seen compare with the one I'm seeing.
As if conversing through our thoughts,
Our spiritual director spoke softly through the loud-speaker.
"Man makes beautiful cathedrals to praise and honor God,
But none as awesome as those God creates for man."
At that moment we were all connected. Amen.

Reflecting to Take Ownership

Bent but Not Broken Tree

Like you, I once stood tall and proud and young,
Believed I was perfectly prepared for
Career, marriage, motherhood.
With a knight in shining armor
To make a reality of my illusions.
Turned out he was not well rooted.
We built our castle on the Pearl of the Caribbean,
But there was no paradise, only lies and tears,
Mocking my faith and culture.
While he selectively embraced
A culture so accepting
Of betrayal and infidelity,

A culture where wives pretended not to see.
But it was engulfing and drowning me.

My faith, my dreams shattered
Tip-toeing on landmines of control and possession,
Abandonment and rejection,
Anger and violence just below the surface,
Convinced me I needed fixing,
Drove me on a lonely one-sided search for solutions.
Oh, once proud and stately tree, I bent and bent.
Until only an empty image stared back in the mirror.
Not the person God created me to be.

From deep within me a voice stirred,
Do not be afraid to leave, to make it on your own.
You will not be alone.
Go, be the woman and mother you want to be.
Return to your faith, regain your pride.
Take your children, raise them right,
They deserve their story full of Light.
But I stayed, one more chance, one more year
Let's get help. Tell me what I need to fix.
"Oh, I am just tired of hearing what a good wife I have.
That everything you do turns out so well.
But, really I just want six months to be free."
He had taken a mistress and more to hide.
"She" was not anonymous,
But someone I hired to work for me.
Oh, what difficult choices lay before me!
To stay and live in despair
With someone who was never there,
Who did not care for wife and children
With love to share,
Or go back to a culture
That shuns singleness and harshly labels you,
A "discarded woman" *"Eres una mujer largada"*.
But one evening watching a happy family on TV,

Seeing a quiet tear run down my face
My children, wise beyond their age said,
"Mom, our dad is not like other dads,
Our family not like other families.
We want you to know
You don't have to stay with him for our sake."
With three suitcases, my children and I left,
Gave him a lifetime to be free.
Papa introduced me to neighbors as "una *mujer largada,*"
But he and Mama took us in," *porque la familia es sagrada*"
My children and I began a new life,
Old friends, bosses and teachers had faith in me.
With God we managed, a team
Together we grew strong and healed.
Money was tight, times were lean.
God provided a roof, food and plain pocket jeans.
Oh, once proud and stately tree,
Rooted in pure mountain springs,
Flowing over rocks warmed by the sun,
Why don't your branches reach the sky?
What bent you down so low?
Was it one big heart-wrenching, gut-tearing blow?
Did someone block your sunshine?
Or constantly uproot you?
Erode the earth below your roots?
Prune your life, tie you down?
Don't tell me, *yo sé que te doblo.*
I know what bent you down so low.
For once I stood tall and proud and strong,
Believed that I could change someone with my love.
Why did I forget where my strength comes from?
Like you, I am bent but not broken,
See, there is New Life in me to guide the Way.
New branches, green and bright, reach up to the Light.
As I continue on my pilgrim's flight.

Finding Redemption and Forgiveness (2014)

Oh, once proud and stately tree
In Holy Land you helped me, a poor pilgrim,
Release my pain, buried silent in my heart.
I am back to Holy Land to
Finish my journey of redemption.
And find forgiveness in my heart, set him free.
Set me free to humbly walk with God forever.
Grateful and at peace.

My Gift of Forgiveness

You are forgiven.
You did not say you're sorry
You did not think you'd hurt me,
Perhaps you do not care
That you did.
I must be concerned about salvation,
Both yours and mine.
So I must forgive you.
Lest I be measured
With my own measure.
I must share in the guilt,
For I ventured into the great big world,
Book smart and street dumb.
Unprepared, without an armor
With which to defend my faith
And stick to my dreams.
I did not turn to God or priest to
Seek sober guidance.
Easy prey in your path.
I must forgive myself.
For following an earthly love
Silencing my conscience.
Yielding to pressure from my culture.
With pride, fear, and hopelessness.

Finding a measure of fulfillment in
Earthly knowledge and accomplishment,
At cost of separating from my faith.
And hurting the One Above.
You don't have to ask for my forgiveness.
You would not understand.
You don't have to value my gift.
It is something I must do.
Only sharing God's gift of mercy
With you.

Pilgrimage of Thanksgiving to the Holy Land

Angels in the Holy Land

One final trip I arranged upon retiring was to the Holy Land in 2005. My brother and sister-in-law told me that when they went they told God, "Now you can let your servants go." I wanted to feel that ready to go to my final destination.

This time I was almost recovered from the chemo and the surgeries and had been cancer free on my check-ups. My blood counts were almost back to normal. God had wanted me to be a grateful survivor on Sacred

Ground. God is pleased when his beloved creatures thank Him. Jesus Christ made it sacred by walking on it for three years, teaching us to get to His Father by following Him. Lord you planned this just for me!!

None of my close friends were coming, but I knew that other people who had been on our two previous trips, would be. I did not choose a roommate because I would be perfectly happy with any of them and excited to get to know someone new, if that is how it worked out. One thing that happens on pilgrimage is that we all become Brothers and Sisters in Christ (B/SIC) by the end of the trip.

I met my fellow pilgrims at the designated gate area at the DFW airport, three hours ahead of time so that we could get our trip bags with the itinerary, get an orientation, and get to know who our room-mate would be. As it turned out, my roommate had been on the Italy trip. I will call her "Angel" because I remembered that she had a smile on her face all the time and snow white hair. I also remembered that she was 83 years old, now 86, had had a fainting spell on our lay-over in Zurich and Loreen had asked me stay with her until the paramedics said she could fly, because of my nursing background. Loreen would arrange for that eventuality if needed. Fortunately, Angel got better just barely in time for us to catch the flight with the group, with me handling both carry-ons and her wheel chair.

Another thing I remembered about Angel, was that she tended to stray from the group, walked looking up, and forgot things back in her room, like cameras, medicine, ID tags, and finally her return ticket two cities back. Luckily, it had been delivered to Loreen just before we'd left. I had even, u-h-m, wondered why her roommate didn't keep better track of her. I vowed to myself that I would do that. At 65 and all healed from surgeries, I was very sure I could do it. She was just a sweet, sweet lady.

With so much of our walking on cobblestoned alleys and streets, and the fact that she had had hip surgery a year back, she did not mind holding on to my arm all the time. Things went well until we went to the Dead Sea. She wanted to go deep enough so that the water would heal her hip. The salt-heavy water was choppy, so I grabbed a plastic chair from the beach and carried it with me into the water explaining to her that she could sit on the chair when the water was deep enough. Wading in the water was a bit difficult, but we finally reached a spot suitable for her purpose. The minute I let go of her and the chair, a wave knocked me over. Water got in my eyes, ears, and nose. Yes, I swallowed some. It took me almost two days to get over the terrible irritation it caused but my sinuses had never felt so clear.

One of the last places we visited was the Temple Mount and the Wailing Wall. I had asked friends and family to send me their petitions and I would ensure that I prayed for them everywhere I went. I typed a list and made several copies to put in the prayer books available at most shrines, and cut one sheet up in strips, to fit in small crags in the Wailing Wall. We were given 20 minutes to visit that site. Angel and I joined hands and said a prayer and I started sticking the papers in the crags. When I noticed that Angel only had one paper to put in, I asked her if she would help me with mine. She was happy to do it and that would keep her close. When we were almost done, she started sobbing. I often react with tears when the Holy Spirit touches me also. I put my arms around her and walked her to the bus. It was almost empty. I held her until she stopped crying.

She opened up to me that on all her trips she asked God for one thing: that she would be able to forgive her best friend who had betrayed her with her husband (as I see it it's the other way around, or just a double betrayal). At 86 she felt she had to forgive her friend before she died. At the wall she had felt a sense of peace and joy and forgiveness. I wondered if I had overwhelmed God with my many petitions, but her joy gave me joy and hope. I said a prayer again for the rest of the petitions and mine.

Petitions in the Wailing Wall

At the hotel I emailed my niece, who had asked her co-workers for their petitions, that I had put all the petitions in the wall that afternoon. After supper I went back to the computer room to check my email and she wanted to know what time I had done it, she would figure the time difference herself. In the morning, she emailed that a co-worker had asked that her daughter, who had been diagnosed with Lupus and had been refusing treatment, at least go see the specialist. At the time I had left the wall, it was morning for them. The daughter woke up before she went to work, dressed to go out, which she had not done since the diagnosis, and asked, "Mom, where is that card for the specialist?"

Weeks later my niece delivered two gifts for me from her co-workers. A second coworker reported that her petition had been for her daughter, who had been diagnosed with advanced Leukemia. Her fiancé had advanced their wedding so that they'd have some time together. She had one treatment and when they did the follow up lab to see if she had responded to it or if they had to adjust it, they had found no sign of Leukemia. They did a repeat test in a month to make sure and again it was negative.

My petitions were answered too, also but not immediately. One was that my cancers would not return. This year I set a daily Mass in gratitude for 18 years as a breast cancer survivor and my 80th birthday. I had asked for good health for my surviving older siblings and a good death for all of us. My oldest brother and I, the youngest, are the only ones still living and we are in good health. He just celebrated his 93rd birthday and I my 80th. I prayed for my children and grandkids. I prayed that I would get closer to God. Every day I give thanks for the many blessings He bestows on me and all the prayers he has answered.

Pilgrimage of Thanksgiving to Holy Land

I did return to the Holy Land a few years ago with my Parish Priest and fellow St. Brigid parishioners in San Antonio. Three of the five members of our SCC, Roses of our Lady, went together. Though, I had not budgeted for that, I felt called to go because my two SCC sisters decided to go. What a great experience for the three of us. Two of us were cancer survivors.

Upon visiting the same site, where mountain springs form the beginning of the Jordan River, I noticed the bent tree thriving, though still bent. I realized something when writing "Bent But Not Broken Tree": I still needed to take ownership for the consequences of my choices. I had been an easy prey on my husband's path. Had I really forgiven him? By not pursuing the divorce, because I did not need that piece of paper, he might have married his mistress sooner. I had not thought about her or her parents' needs to see her union at least legitimized. Her mother who lived three houses from the factory had actually let me know before I left PR, that she did not approve of "all that's going on." I had not set him free here on earth. Perhaps I had deflected or rationalized that I was the only victim.

He had in fact told me when my daughter flew him in to meet her children that he had married her a year after the divorce, because her father had begged him on his death bed to marry her! He had also come as close to telling me he was sorry as that poor soul was capable of, "You all have done really well for yourselves without me. Perhaps you would not be as well off, if I had been in the picture."

I added the last verses to the poem, for my own closure of that leg of my journey of faith.

Roses of Our Lady SCC in Holy Land

Reflection:

1. Is there something in my life that I have to give closure to?

2. Is there something I must own and forgive myself for?

3. Do I consciously consider that my actions may have an impact on another's life, be an occasion for their sin or for their salvation even?

9
COMMUNITY

~ ·)(· ~

Carry Your Own Weight

The "*dichos*" or sayings of a people portray who they are, what the culture is that guides their actions. My parents' sayings and actions guided me in serving God and neighbor.

"If you extend your hand out, let it be to lift someone up."

"If you give someone a drink, don't give them half a cup."

"Our enemies are also created by God. They deserve respect and "a please and a thank you, a greeting and a blessing."

"Your friends get the same, but you shake their hand, pat their back or hug them."

"If you honk at the goose flying ahead of you, let it be in encouragement."

"Tell me who you're with and I will tell you who you are."

One saying that I believe orders family life, work life, and even the whole of society is "Carry your own weight and a bit of somebody else's."

In our family there was seldom any liquid cash. People did things for each other according to their skills and bartered this for that. Usually with a little more pitched in either way. If my father trained a horse for someone or taught them how to slaughter an animal and process its meat, and the hide, he might come home with a bushel of onions and/or carrots and/or limes. My mother sewed clothes and even made her own patterns. She might get some money and a stack of flour cloth sacks of the same color or print. She made artificial flower wreaths and arrangements for The Day of the Dead, Mother's Day, Veterans Day, etc. for people to place on the tomb of loved one. Payments were made in the same way. The vases always returned for her to re-use.

"Carry your own weight and a bit of someone else's meant that we were a family team, with individual chores, common chores like setting the table, cleaning up after a dust storm, hanging clothes on the lines to dry, harvesting the crops. Unpleasant chores like cleaning the outhouse and putting lime in the pit was each user's responsibility, held accountable by the next user. One kid cleaned the chicken coop and gathered eggs, another cleaned the angora rabbits' cages and fed them and so on. If you did not feel like doing your chore, you might barter with your sibling to trade. No use involving your parents or complaining.

You carried your own weight by taking care of yourself, your clothes, and your bed and did your chores, which was always praised. "You can always count on Rene to carry his own weight." But you also helped each other when you needed more than one pair of hands, or someone had an exam or got sick.

This also meant that you kept your yard, and the area in front of your house free of weeds and garbage. You helped clean the church, the cemetery before Dia de los Muertos, the school before classes started and after they ended, and after a dust storm during the semester. You helped widows and disabled or elderly people.

My parents were proud to say that even after the depression they had not relied on public assistance. People shared their rations and recipes to at least vary the flavor of the processed meats they got.

Carry your weight at work meant do an honest day's work, work fast and efficiently. Be loyal to your employer, do more than required if you wanted to get ahead or a raise.

One saying and how my parents were called to stand by it, made me mad. "Let every man have his song." My mother had had several fundraisers to fix the cloth ceiling of the church when it started sagging and dropping animal sediment on the pews. She kept the money in a small empty paint pail. It was stolen and they knew who did it. It was a young man who was often drunk. He'd come to our house and waited for my brother to come home. We all went about our chores not paying attention to him. He finally left before my brother came.

My mother discovered the money was gone from the pail, shortly after, when someone came to make a contribution.

They decided not to notify the parents or expose the young man because it would bring shame to their family. That would take away their song. My mother made another quilt to raffle off and set another dance.

The Day the River Took Too Much

Three families came from California, daughter and son with spouses, granddaughter and husband with a great-grandchild on the way. They scrimped and saved in bittersweet anticipation of gathering with family at the five-year anniversary Mass of their mother's death, my father's sister. Adults shared childhood memories of happier Easter celebrations on the Banks of the Rio Grande aka Rio Bravo.

Not much happens or changes in that in that isolated old Spanish settlement that the rest of Texas and the nation have left behind. The only industry is farming small remnants of ancestral Spanish land grants, three bars, and two grocery stores with gas pumps in one of them, and a pool hall. Younger people who have a job have to commute to Roma or Rio Grande. The only way other people travel is to do migrant work. The people, though sixth or seventh generations Americans, cling to blended traditions and customs, food and music, faith and language of Spain and Mexico.

You can break the cycle of poverty only if you leave for a better education or jobs or enlist in the Army, or to seek adventure and freedom from customs and expectations that bind, but you are always drawn back. Those who make it out there bring their younger sibling up, or the whole family. Many have returned after they retire and build homes that stand out from the others.

One thing had changed for our village that those three families were not aware of or were not conscious of the impact. The Falcon Dam had been built and completed about seven miles upriver. Now the flow and amount of water that went downriver was a blessing for residents and farmers. Controlled well timed water flow for daily needs and crops. Flooding was no longer a concern. But occasionally the gates were open wider to release more water, either to prevent flooding upland or relieve drought down river. On the day before the Mass, three family members drowned in the river, one with her unborn child because the dam gates were opened at that moment, creating strong currents. A siren is sounded as warning. Perhaps no one told them what it meant.

The people who live day to day from the land, who barter crops for goods and services, whose hands seldom exchange money, responded. They rallied to meet the grave tragedy head on. They volunteered to search for the bodies. Three caskets were bought with donations, were prayed over at church, and followed in procession the short distance to the cemetery. They prepared abundant food for the reception back at the church, for many of us came to their funeral from out of town, and donated cash.

Three funeral plots and graves opened, paid for with donations and labor. Our families consoled, blessed, prayed for, and three returned to California with food and gas money to get them safely back, grieving the three that drowned. The community grieved with them and the tragedy remains part of the lore of the quiet village.

More signs were added by the county: Warning, Strong Currents. Siren Will Sound.

No signs are needed: Warning: Strong Bonds in this town, they will always draw you back.

Sheltering the Oppressed

Isaiah 58:1-9a *This, rather, is the fasting that I wish: sheltering the oppressed and the homeless; Clothing the naked when you see them, and not turning your back on your own.*

You ask me to shelter the oppressed, Lord.
This requires courage to go against the current.
Climbing down from my pedestal; take risks.
Who are the oppressed, Lord?
Aren't we all oppressed by the world?
Aren't we all seeking a safe haven and acceptance?
Aren't we all dragged down by feelings of being
Down-trodden, demoralized, exploited?

I look around and listen.
I see the immigrant, the refugee.
The poor, the under-educated, under-employed,
The ones with extra color on their skin,
The ones burdened with addictions,
The ones who've lost a grip on reality,
Wise ones with furrows and wrinkles on their faces,
The one in the mirror.

What can I do, Lord?
Where do I begin?
Shall I listen with my heart?
Look them in the eye and smile,
Extend my hand as a lifeline or embrace them.
Be their voice.
Walk in their shoes,
Fast and share my gifts.

Is that enough, Lord?
Is that pleasing to you, Lord?

Thou Shall Not Kill

With the simplicity of a child, when I was learning the Ten Commandments from the Catechism from Mama, she said we were to obey them because they came from God. She told us how God gave them to Moses in two stone tablets. I was certain I would always obey the Sixth Commandment. I would never stab, shoot or mortally injure a human being. In fact I would not even do that to an animal.

As an adult I learned many other applications of "thou shall not kill, and of the overriding "thou shall love thy neighbor as yourself" commandment. What about "killing" someone's spirit, reputation, their standing in the community or in their workplace, or among their peers with gossip, slander, or parents telling a kid they will never amount to anything? I realized protecting life, which is part of the mandate, is not always easy. What about not paying a just wage to a whole group of people based on the color of their skin? Forcing them to live in poverty, or to work two jobs to make ends meet, does that not kill or diminish them or their family life or their health? What about the practice of "assisted death" which is becoming more commonplace?

In the early 1990's, I volunteered with Dallas Area Interfaith Council doing workshops for unemployed persons at different host churches. One day, without explanation, they sent me to present the workshop at an office complex instead. When I arrived, I saw pro-life picketers praying in front of an abortion clinic nestled between business offices! I also saw uniformed policemen and their guns and handcuffs at the ready. I started sobbing uncontrollably, as I set up for the workshop in a conference room upstairs from it.

The presence of evil was oppressive. Visions of the praying picketers made me question my own commitment to protect life. Did my fear of policemen, Rangers, Border Patrol agents and their guns, the result of witnessing them as a child treat all migrant workers or even my father, a sixth generation American, working in his own fields, unjustly, keep me from joining protesters or was it just my own cowardice or shallow commitment to my own beliefs?

Suddenly sounds of sobs coming from the stairwell nearby, penetrated my consciousness. I followed the sound a few feet down the hallway to an Exit door. I found a young couple sitting on the stairs, crying and clinging to each other, the girl obviously pregnant. I did not want to intrude, but felt led to them. *Lord, what can I tell them? Will they tell me to mind my own business?*

The Holy Spirit spoke through me, "I don't mean to intrude, but you are obviously faced with a very tough decision. Have you spoken to a friend or a minister you trust?" They were speechless, so I continued "Have you heard of Hope Cottage? They help you explore all your options. If the mother decides to have the baby but give it up for adoption, they provide shelter and medical care until the baby is born. They provide more services to the mother after birth and adoption. If you choose to stay connected to your child through the adopting parents, the agency ensures they find adoptive parents who will agree to allow that."

I sensed their hope when they stopped sobbing. Luckily, I had grabbed my purse when I left the empty room, so I pulled out a business card for Hope Cottage, I gave directions and the name of another contact person in case the one on the card was not there. They walked to the exit door, pausing to look back at me wide eyed, before rushing down the stairs, still unable to speak.

Earlier in the week, the United Way Budget Allocation Panel which I chaired, had met with the Board of Directors and management staff of Hope Cottage, as part of the funding process. We had noted that Open Adoptions were going down and the funds from United Way were not effectively utilized. We asked them to consider offering both Open and Closed adoptions as options to mothers. We would not cut their funding until we could observe results for a couple of years.

Returning to the room, I explained what had happened to the people now waiting for the workshop to begin. They said they figured I was around since the room was set up. A man asked "What were they wearing?" I described their clothes, adding "They are just kids." He said "They didn't do it! I saw them getting in a car and drive away. I thought it odd she was still pregnant."

They said they also felt uncomfortable being in this place and asked if we could just cancel the workshop. We said a prayer for the young couple, every mother undergoing an abortion and the ones providing the abortion services. We prayed for the unborn, denied a right to life. On the way out we encouraged the pro-life picketers.

Reflection:

1. Do I stay silent in the face of a need to intervene or help, because of fear of "intruding"?

2. Are there other ways beside picketing, demonstrations, etc., I can support a cause or protest an injustice?

3. Where do I stand on abortion or other issues? Am I obligated to take a stand?

Community — Another Way of Being Church

Small Faith Sharing Groups
(AKA Small Christian Communities) – Dallas

Acts 2:37-47 Those who accepted his message were bap-tized, and about three thousand persons were added that day. They devoted themselves to the teaching of the apostles and to the communal life, to the breaking of the bread and to the prayers Awe came upon everyone, and many wonders and signs were done through the apos-tles. All who believed were together and had all things in common; they would sell their property and posses-sions and divide them among all according to each one's need. Every day they devoted themselves to meeting together in the temple area and to breaking bread in their homes. They ate their meals with exultation and sincerity of heart, praising God and enjoying favor with all the people. And every day the Lord added to their number those who were being saved.

Early in 1991, when my pastor at Holy Trinity Church in Dallas called me to ask if I would help him organize Small Faith Sharing Groups in the church, I told him I did not know what they were. He reassured me that he would teach me all I needed to know about them. He'd recognized me on TV speaking on behalf of my employer, Dallas Area Rapid Transit, and had learned that I was over Human Resources. He said, "DART Lady, you must have management and organizing skills. That's what I need."

I learned that these groups were promoted in Vatican II as a way of going back to basics in the Catholic Church, like Prisca and Aquila and Lydia. Acts 2: 37-47 describes life for Christianity at its inception. They actually are called by many names, the most common and accurate is "Small Christian (or Church) Communities (SCCs)."

Holy Trinity is an inner city parish, known for its early inclusion of the LGBT community nearby, mixed with artists, parishioners from a very affluent area on one side, middle class multi-unit housing with some Section 8 units occupied by mostly Hispanic/Latino immigrants, but also Croatian and Serbian refugees and immigrants from other war ravaged countries, and Mexican Americans on another side. There are professional and other workers who work in the downtown area, but live elsewhere, like me. We formed 44 Small Faith Sharing Groups of English and Spanish language preferences for sharing. We trained English and Spanish speaking group leaders, facilitators and hosts, and facilitators for quarterly networking meetings. Our priest suggested that we all do the Little Rock study series of Saints' lives and we obtained the books in English and Spanish.

There is something very spiritual about a people of faith, praying, taking a retreat, or having the same experience in solidarity at the same time. It may be that people join individually, like joining where ever you are to do the Angelus at noon and at 3 PM, or in a small group to do a novena for peace, with groups all over the nation or world doing the same thing. Our Lord bestows many blessings on the home and family that hosts a group in His name. Heaven is flooded with love, prayers and petitions. God responds.

I joined one of the groups and met with them for ten years until I retired and moved to San Antonio, Texas. Learning about the saints, examining their life as modeling an exemplary Christian life, incorporating at least some of their spiritual habits into our own can be very transformational. The dynamics in the group itself spur the members to discover their gifts and to use them for the good of all. They then strengthen the life of parish.

I made life-long friends, who can stay at my home and I can stay at theirs. When I first moved to San Antonio, for several years I had company from Dallas during Fiesta. When I had cancer, I had not yet developed a circle of friends in San Antonio. In fact we were just forming the Core Team at St. Brigid to form Small Christian Communities when I had surgery for cancer. My son was still in Dallas and came to help his sister take care of me Wednesday evening to Sunday evening. My friends took time off their jobs to come with him and help him take care of me for three weekends, until I could get around on my own.

Small Christian Communities – San Antonio

I became involved with various ministries at St. Brigid, but missed my Dallas SCC dearly. I was participating in an Alpha course in August 2002 when a new Adult Faith Formation Director was hired. She came to introduce herself and to get to know the people in the parish. When she said, "I will help you in all that you do already, but my hope is that that some of you will have a passion for Small Christian Communities, or as they are known in Latin America *Pequeñas Comunidades de Base.*" I wrote a note and handed it to her before she walked out, "I organized Small Faith Sharing Groups in Dallas and have been wishing I could find one to join here in SA. Would love to help."

Within a few months we had formed a Core Team, of which I was Co-coordinator and then Coordinator, until three years ago. We had sign-ups and formed 10 SCCs. We invited new communities to form after every parish-based retreat or course. Currently we have 23 SCCs at St. Brigid and I am a member of two, *which is not recommended*, one shares in English and the other in Spanish. After sixteen years of forming, nourishing and networking the SCCs, I identified some great leaders in "branching" a SCC, The Gospel Gang, which grew to 23 adult members and 27 children in four years, with a waiting list of couples wanting to join them! They remembered that in forming them I had mentioned "branching" into two or more SCCs in such a circumstance. I turned the leadership over to a new, younger person, and helped her form a new Core Team. They retained me as an SCC Ambassador and assure me I will always be their OG. (No, not Old Goat, Original Gospel Gang, because I formed them and re-formed them.) Most of the new SCCs now forming consist of young couples with children, so that made more sense to turn over the Coordinator role to younger people.

It was in San Antonio that I started seeking other SCCS locally and nationally to network with. I attended a National Convocation of SCCs in St. Paul, MN and met leaders of three organizational sponsors of the Convocation and many members from all over the states and some even from abroad. The possibilities are mind-boggling of how to form SCCs, what resources to use in forming, nourishing and net-working them, and on-going material to use in the groups' meetings.

There is no one way to do SCCs, and it seems that each group finds out what works for them. But it is important to get them started on the same foot and maintain them connected to a parish. The first experience is more long-lasting if it is well organized and impactful.

SCCs, (they are called by over 200 different names, have certain things in common, in what they are and what they do.

+ They are structurally connected to a parish.

+ A small group of 10-12 people who meet in homes several times a month. Weekly or every other week is the ideal. The roles of host and facilitator of the meetings are rotated among the members.

+ Usually are lectionary based, discussing the scriptures for the following Sunday, in a structured format, with an aim of connecting God's work to their daily life through study, reflection and sharing life and faith experiences. Some vary the resources they use like reading and discussing a Catholic based book.

+ Break bread in fellowship, with light snacks or meal.

+ God's Word calls us to act on it, individually or as a group, reaching out in times of need or adversity. Most members join one or two ministries in the parish.

+ They Evangelize.

Over the thirty years I have been involved with SCCs in Dallas and San Antonio, and globally through our website: smallchristriancommunities.org, and a SKYPE SCC, I have witnessed that membership in a SCC transforms your life in many ways but, primarily:

+ Your faith is strengthened and you increase your knowledge of Catholic/Christian beliefs and increase your worship time in activities beside Mass.

+ You discover your God-Given gifts and how to use them for the good of all and to act in service to others.

✦ You are called to evangelize and witness to others.

✦ We support, encourage and hold each other accountable in our faith journey.

✦ You build close and lasting friendships with others with same beliefs and goals as yours. The friendship shared in the groups becomes a very powerful antidote against isolation.

✦ You become a better version of yourself (parent, spouse, brother, sister, neighbor, etc.)

It was in the SCCs that I became truly aware of the Holy Spirit, the Third Person of our Triune God. I learned who He is and what He does. I learned to seek Him in my life, in nature and to make others aware of Him. Many others have shared the same thing with me. In networking meetings of all the SCCs, we give an opportunity to members to share how their life has been transformed. Some common examples:

✦ Love takes on a "face" and provides "the snowshoe effect" where the weight of an individual's burden is distributed to and lightened by the Community's love and prayers. One example was that the members visit and pray for members who were ill or dying, even across SCCs.

✦ We discovered greater ways to live our faith because of the support and encouragement that was experienced in the group.

✦ The children of group members may be in a back room playing or watching a video, but they eat and pray with the adults at the end. The children see the importance of these groups to their parents, and feel they too were "part of a larger very special family" – one that was clearly Christ centered. One Youth SCC has formed and has already undertaken several projects in the Parish.

SCC Gospel Gang III Commitment Ritual

10

Close To Nature –
Close To God

TREES

Trees tell me secrets.
How their roots feel earth's
heartbeat.
Their crests high above,
Touch the clouds, and they
Whisper of God's love.
They survive harsh winds,
drought and cold.
Those things do not touch their
inner core,
Nor shape their soul.

Trees Tickling the Clouds

Waves at Cape Cod Beach

WAVES

Waves tell me their adventures
As they wander between heaven and earth,
And from shore to shore.
They beckon me to come with them,
To build up another shore.
Assure me they always bring back what they take.
Remind me that the beach survives their battering
Because it yields.
Thus they witness resiliency.

Blue Heron Flying into the Sunset

Sunrise/Sunset

Sunrises and sunsets speak
Of beginnings and endings.
For that is how it must be:
Release the hurt
Make way for healing.
A setting sun signals day's end,
Time for rest that refreshes and renews.
The sunrise heralds
God's gift of new day,
To be received,
Cherished and shared.

Hurricanes

Romans 8:22 *We know that the whole creation has been groaning as in the pains of childbirth right up to the present time, aging earth and universe.*
Jeremiah 12:11 *It has been made a desolation, Desolate, it mourns before me; the whole land has been made desolate, because no man lays it to heart.*

Hurricanes, wind and raging waters
Waging desolation and destruction,
Not only man's structures
But God's own creation.

Mighty majestic trees down,
Their hearts and arteries severed.
Shores violated and oceans catapulted
Upon the land.

Your anger, Lord, is justified
Wisdom ordered the chaos of the universe
But man is bent on tainting and spoiling this land
It must seem to you that man has lost your heart.

Values ignored in self interest
Truth altered to shroud decaying souls.
Your sons worshipping false idols,
Leaders corrupted by power, superiority and greed.

Yet we stand courageous in outrage,
United our charity, love and hope prevail.
To pull each other out of
Disheartening obliteration.

Redeem us anew, Lord.
We will calm your creation,
Renew our temporary home
Into your sacred temple.

Our Universe in Tears

1 Thes 4:13 *Do not grieve as others do who have no hope.*

We pray for near and dear ones who suffer.
Our hearts are moved when loved ones weep.
But do our prayers reach across the oceans
For those ravished by war, violence and hunger?

Our God is a loving God, embracing all who love him.
But do we love brothers and sisters whose suffering we do not see?
Hardly a thought or a prayer
For those who risk their lives for every Eucharist received.

Our universe is witness to their tears.
But it groans and cries for future children
As we waste, destroy and contaminate our temporary home,
That must serve God's people to the end of time.

Not a tear for those not given a chance to life.
Not a care for those who will come after us.
We know them not, because we see them not.
Are they not also made in God's own image?

Our God is a loving God.
The universe his gift for us to share.
Not to harm by thoughtless care.
That at our journey's end
We'll all find Him there.

From Grapes to Grace

Tenderly grown
In chosen Pure Soil.
Formed in mystery.
In Cana gently cast
By Mother Mary
To start your ministry.
Unlike the grape
You did foresee your destiny
To fulfill ancient prophecies.

You were pulled
Crushed, bruised
Scourged, pressed to a tree.
In dark place aged three days
To grace Holy altar.
Before Communities
Of brothers and sisters,
Obedient to your command
In memory of You.

No longer grape but redeeming grace
For countless generations
In every nation,
Through the end of time.
To partake in community
With brothers and sisters
Through Holy Eucharist
Worthy to claim your promise
To share your heavenly space.

Come Into My Garden

Jerusalem Garden

Come through the gate
Leave behind anger and hate
Sit on my bench and rest
Shed your worries and fears
Visit with me a while.

Now that your soul is fed
Let your heart be filled
With love and peace
My child, be still
Sit with me a while.

11

FAITH IN THE PUBLIC ARENA

My Country Tis' the Colors That I See

USA Flag

My Country, you are freedom
Tis' not your flag of
Red, White and Blue,
For other countries fly the same,
Yet their citizens are not free.
My Country, you are welcoming

Of the poor, the persecuted, and the
Victims of war ravaged areas.
You welcome the people that
From other countries flee.
My Country, tis' the colors that I see
In the streets a-bustle.
Industrious bold faces of brown, black,
Yellow, red and white and
Blended hues in between.
Proof that truly, my Country is
A stew of many flavors.
All working to make you great.
Enriching all of society
With diverse cultures, faith, food and dress.
All investing in your fate.
My Country, founded in God's law,
We weave your colors with our faith.
We are a beacon on the hill for all to see
Strong and united we stand against
Those who would divide us,
Diminish our institutions
And weaken the values we stand for.
May our country endure forever.

Am I Invisible?

Jelly Fish

I am invisible to you,
Or you see me through your own prism,
So I'm only a projection of your intake.
Truth is, you see me now,
Speaking for my employer
Carrying their public relations
Message or information
For bilingual audiences.
Ever wonder how I got here?
How painfully poor I was growing up?
See the butterflies in my stomach.
You see me and close your little circle
On me at a civic event or Chamber meeting.
I'm the brunt of your displeasure
At their past neglect;
No one knew your language,
Or went home at 5 PM.

I'm only building good will for my public employer
And informing you of business opportunities.
Not part of my job, but the ones with the power

Don't speak the language and
Have gone home.
Why do you not see that I care for community?
And for small minority owners eager to
Get public contracts and prosper?
Do you know I once was a small business owner,
Striving to get government contracts?

Do you know that I'm the thorn on their conscience?
Who gives you a voice in the internal decision making?
That the general clause of our job description that says
"Be responsible stewards of the public trust."
Is seldom defined or interpreted as
"Give back to the community that pays your salary."
See me here when others go home.

My Life Cycle of Faith

When you don't have much, your hope is your prayer.
To someday work upright
Out of blazing sun and dusty cotton fields.
You hope to break the cycle of poverty,
To rest alone in a real bed,
For more than one pair of shoes, store bought dresses,
A dust free home with running water to drink and bathe.

You know there is a better life
From books you read in school,
The Sears Catalog and radio.
Your parents have hopes for you too.
Be a good person, pray to Diosito, get *una educación*.
You will get out of blue denim.

You pray for good grades, a college degree, and a career.
Someone to share your life with,
Marriage, children, your own home.
The world says you need more, the latest car, perfumes.
You surround yourself with more things and activities, more more
Memories of poverty, hard labor and dust yet endure.

One day you begin to pray for others: your kids, grandkids friends,
and the hungry, for those ravaged by wars, the sick
and for the unborn. You pray for things you cannot see or touch.
For closeness, for wholeness, for purpose and peace of mind.
You pray for greater faith, to feel God's love, to get closer to God.
A walk in unspoiled nature to feel God's presence.

Without knowing when it happened or how long you've felt it,
You feel complete and your heart is joyful.
No longer hungry, no longer seeking, no longer reaching.
You're certain He was with you in the dusty cotton fields.
Will be there at the end of your journey.
You pray in simple gratitude.

THE END

About the Author

B elza Ramos was born in 1940 in Salineño, Starr Co., TX, a tiny community by the Rio Grande River. At fifteen, she moved with her parents to Corpus Christi, Texas. They joined her five older siblings already living there. The move opened up opportunities of better schools, colleges and universities, where she could pursue her dream of being a nurse. Belza's life is full of "firsts" as a Hispanic woman with roots in a migrant worker family. In an era when there were few Hispanic or Hispanic women role models, she was first in her family to graduate from college, became a professional nurse, a manufacturing entrepreneur and finally retired as an Assistant Vice President–Human Resources from the Dallas Area Rapid Transit Authority. She has been listed in the National Association of Female Executives and was a Founding and Board member of The National Association of Public Sector EEO Officers. Throughout her career and civic involvement she advocated for equal opportunity and equity in pay for women and people of color, and equal rights for all.

Why I Write

I write stories of growing up when God, family and country marked the moral compass points of our lives. I want to encourage our youth to get a good basic education that will provide flexibility to switch or forge new careers should their life situation change or in the event of economic downturns or technological advances which make their skills obsolete. In my own life I did not plan it that way but it all worked very well for me. I tell young people to focus on what they want to try first. Your faith in God and in yourself, your skills and personal attributes always go with you. After surviving experiences with cancer, my writing has been more faith –based. Now that I'm retired I pursue other interests besides writing: reading, photography, drawing and painting. My goal is lifelong learning, staying healthy, and active so I can enjoy my family and friends. When I write with the hindsight of an adult, I understand life better. **And I get to laugh and cry all over again!!**